The Inner Guide Meditation

A contemporary classic that synthesizes insights from Tarot, astrology, the Qabalah, alchemy and analytical psychology to create a powerful system of self-transformation and enlightenment.

The Inner Guide Meditation

by

Edwin C. Steinbrecher

THE AQUARIAN PRESS
Wellingborough, Northamptonshire

First published in the United Kingdom 1982
Second Impression 1983

British Library Cataloguing in Publication Data

Steinbrecher, Edwin C.
  The Inner Guide Meditation.
  1. Meditation
  I. Title
  158'.12   BL627

ISBN 0-85030-300-1

Printed and bound in Great Britain.

Contents

List of Illustrations

Acknowledgements

Grateful acknowledgement is made to Inner Traditions International, Ltd., 377 Park Avenue South, New York, NY 10016; Oxford University Press, 200 Madison Avenue, New York, NY 10016; Princeton University Press, Princeton, NJ 08540; and to the Sabian Publishing Society, 2324 Norman Road, Stanwood, WA98292 for their permissions to utilize materials from their respective publications.

I would also like to thank the following people and groups who have helped in their many and varied ways to produce this present work. My thanks to my parents, Edwin E. and Helen S. Steinbrecher, my God-mother, Josephine Siska, the real Founder of D.O.M.E., my three known Inner Guides, Aman, George and Ta, Kirsten Dehner Abel, the American Federation of Astrologers, Theodora Anderson, The Aquarian Press Limited, Dolores Ashcroft-Nowicki, the Astrological Guild of New Mexico, Astro Numeric Service, Annie Ausland, Bren Bacon, David E. Bacon, Dee and Dale Barber, Jo Ann Barone, Jean Bayliss, Cary F. Baynes, Ben Bedford, Sandia Belgrade, David Philip Benge, Muriel Berman, Graham Binette, Nick Blaisdell, Blue Feather Press, Giovanni and Maria Teresa Boni, Maggie, David and Teddy Bott, Millie Bradley, *Brain/Mind Bulletin*, Laura Breska, Mary Anne Brinson, Joan Buresch, Al and Judy Burnett, Fred Buttrell, Gary Callaway, Virginia Campbell, Carlos Castaneda, Paul Foster Case, Frank Clark, John E. Clerkin, Jr., Diana Coe, Charlotte Colorado, Tamara Comstock, John Cooper-Walker, Cathleen, Michael, Ruth and Stephen P. Connors, Bob and Judy Carr Conrad, Ellie and Francis Ford Coppola, Doris Cross, Aleister Crowley, Edith Custer and *The Mercury Hour*, William M. Davidson, Doris and Larry Davis, Dell *Horoscope*, Peter Del

Monte (Beech), Lynn Derhak, Lola Douglas-Howard, Bruce Drake, Faye Dunaway, Jean Dunaway, Joan and James Easly, Arni and Dorette Egilsson, Freemont Ellis II, Thyrza Escobar-Jones, Jean Faivus, Tres Feltman, Gary Finnell, Dion Fortune, Julie Fox, George Freeman, Kathy Freeman, Bill and Kris Gallegos, Bob and Anne Garner, Janet Garth, Bob Gathers, Markham C. Godwin, Bette and Sid Greenberg, Norma Gremore, Pat Griffin, Joan Hackett, John Hall of Helios Books, Catherine Harlé, Jack B. Harrington, Ben Harris, Maryanne Hastings, Jack B. Heatherton, Steven Hechter, Lon Hill and family, Megen Lloyd Hill, Frances Hillin, Hal Hodges, Dale M. Holmen, Mary Holmes, Hospice of Boulder, Colorado, Gretta L. Howell, Rosalie Howland, Carol Huff-stickler, Hallie Iglehart, John Immel, Sabine Jacob, Sue James, Jesus of Nazareth, Marc Edmund Jones, Carl G. Jung, Jerry Kay, Arthur Kennedy, Dorothy Kimbell, Tom and Virginia Kirby and family, James Kirsch, Gareth Knight, W. A. von Koch, David Krantz, Elisabeth Kübler-Ross, Lama Foundation, Nathaniel Lande, Lao Tzu, Charles W. Leadbeater, V. Louise Leak, Robert E. and Mary Lee, Georgene Leopold, John C. Lilly, Katharine Lockwood, Jackie and Monica Lustgarten, Fabio and Marco Macchioni, Bob and Sara Mack, Helen Matlock, Tom and Joan McCullough, Greg McFarland, Philip T. McGowan, R. Michael McGowan, Steve McQueen, Sally Mehalek, Pavita Miller, Sue Miller, Jack Mobley, Raymond A. Moody, Jr., Holly Hughes Morelli, Tootie Morgan, Teri Mullen, Mary Navratil, Howard and Jean Newcomb, the New York Astrology Centre, Patty Markov Nicholson, F. Richard Nolle, Bill and Peggy Norton, Maji Oberne, Kevin O'Neal, Maile Orme, Jim and Ralph Oswald, Paracelsus, Para Research, Stan Parker, the Leigh Peacocke family, Portia Moyers, Bob Pike, the Pinon Fast Print staff, Plato, Jerry Plunkett, Richard Polese, Margot Pomeroy, Geraldine Price, Marty Priest, Pythagoras, Cherokee Quintana, Ram Dass, Suzanne Gross Reed, F. Israel Regardie, Linda Richards, Edwin Rivera, Jane Marla Robbins, Lois M. Rodden, Carol Rogers, Basil Rokóczi, Lillian Romero, Steve Rosen-blum, Betty Ross, Sheila W. Ross, Karel Ruekert, Joel Salisbury, Linda Salisbury, Robin Saltsman, Coe and Galen Savage, Paula Jan Holland Schimmel, Isha and R. A. Schwaller de Lubicz, Murray D. Scott, Doris Senutovitch, Julia M. Seton, Tony Shearer, Talia Shire, Pamela Marks Silberer, Alex

Silberstein, Caroline Simpson, Craig Siska, Frank and Blanche Siska, Frank Siska, Jr., James Siska, Josepha Siska, Shirley Siska, Merrie E. Smith, Patricia E. Smith, Socrates, Mary Lynn and Neils Sorenson, Lisa and Ehud C. Sperling, Margaret Starr, Dan Stat, Charles and Mary Steinbrecher, Lynn and Kristen Steinbrecher, Martin and Debi Steinbrecher, Roy and Judy Steinbrecher, Elizabeth Stephenson, Audrey Stone, Sheila Sullivan, Susan and Joshua Swartzberg, Samuel W. Swedenborg, Karl T. and Holly Tani and family, Gwyneth Taylor, Mark Taylor, Leigh Taylor-Young, Gia Terry, Willoughby Thorn, Sharon and Jack Timmer, Simca Torah, Tsuki, Debbie Trissel and family, the U.C.L.A. Art Department and Students' Store, Cleo Dovolos Usher, Aurelio Valdez, Jr., Theodora Van Runkle, Elizabeth Dunlap Verplank, Abbé N. de Villars, Richard John Vratanina, Camille Waters, Marty Weil, Bradford Weston, Jim Wheelock, Jr., Maris Whitaker, Richard Wilhelm, Rosalind Greenberg Wholden, John Garrett Woodsmall, Charles Woodworth, Georgene Wyatt, Anna Maria and Norman Zimmerman.

'Then he moved on, and I behind him followed' (engraving by
Gustave Doré from Dante's *Inferno*).

Foreword

When I received the 1977 edition of *The Guide Meditation,* I was very much impressed by the lucidity of instruction and synthesizing practicality of Edwin Steinbrecher's text. A practical method of developing the techniques of the visual imagination outside the heated confines of the psychologist's consulting room or the occult lodge is urgently needed for a new generation of seekers after the ancient wisdom.

   Edwin Steinbrecher's approach could well be an important contribution to the expression of the Mysteries of the Age of Aquarius.

GARETH KNIGHT

'We each possess an inner liberator, who will release us from our chains' (engraving by Gustave Doré from The Bible).

Preface to the Fifth Edition

Despite both private and small printings, *The Inner Guide Meditation* has found and continues to find its way all over the world and to many diverse peoples through some sort of spiritual grapevine that both carries and endorses it, seeing that it reaches those ready and eager to work with their Inner Guides. I thank Spirit in all Its Manifestations for this.

The new discoveries and knowledge achieved through work with the Guides seems endless, and, as each edition is revised and added to, I feel much like a man polishing a gem to enable it to reflect and refract more Light.

May the book continue to reach and touch the lives of all those who have asked for such a way to journey within.

Love, Light and Freedom to you all.

EDWIN C. STEINBRECHER
D.O.M.E.
The Inner Guide Meditation Center
P.O. Box 25358
Colorado Springs, Colorado 80936
USA.
January 1983

Preface to the Fourth Edition

More than a year has passed since the publications of the Third Edition of *The Guide Meditation*. It is to be remembered that this is an infant meditation, just nine years old now, and it keeps continually revealing new aspects of itself, requiring adjustments of previously held concepts and assimilation of the vast wealth of information constantly emerging.

I have attempted to add those concepts which I feel are necessary for the understanding of where we are now in Time, this last phase of the Piscean vibration before reality turns a corner and we enter Aquarius.

It is a period when meditation, meditation of any kind, is our necessity. Meditate yourselves, and encourage all you know to meditate in whatever way is comfortable or useful for them.

Love, Light and Freedom to you all.

EDWIN C. STEINBRECHER
October 1978

Turn inward for your voyage!
For all your arts,
You will not find the Stone
In foreign parts.

Angelus Silesius, Alchemist

THE INNER GUIDE MEDITATION

Part 1

'The Kingdom of Heaven is *truly* within you and your Guide will show you your way' (engraving by Gustave Doré from Dante's *Paradise*).

'Wise men follow the stars' (Engraving by Gustave Doré from The Bible).

Introduction

The Inner Guide Meditation is the product of the mingling of a number of spiritual and philosophical streams: astrology, tarot, alchemy, analytical psychology, qabalah and the Western Mystery Tradition, which contains the Judaeo-Graeco-Christian spiritual heritage of the West. From this synthesis of potent currents comes a gestalt in which the Guides – humanity's lost teachers – appear, fresh, alive and waiting to serve the individual spiritual quest; to lead us toward the 'Kingdom of Heaven' to be found within each of us. The Inner Guide Meditation is a transformative process concerned with assimilating the disparate energies which exist in the human unconscious into the unified wholeness that is the awakened, enlightened being inherent in each of us, thus ending the illusions which cause separation, guilt, and judgement. With the mediation of the Inner Guides, problems once unapproachable and unchangeable become fulfilling challenges that bring forth productive and creative life responses.

Astrology provides the only available 'road map' of the inner and outer worlds. An astrological chart diagrams the multi-dimensional physics of the unconscious and shows the structural relationships among the reality-creating, reality sustaining energies each of us carries. The tarot provides images akin to these energies, and forms that contain and present aspects of the living energies of God and the universe, so that our individual egos can experience them and comprehend them. Alchemy and analytical psychology furnish us with processes and concepts through which we can assimilate these particular energies, allowing us to understand and incorporate within ourselves the living substance of our individual world perceptions. The qabalah and the Western

Mystery Tradition give us time-tested tools with which to work and experiment in the inner dimensions. And our Inner Guides give us the teaching, guidance and necessary protection as we follow the path of our individual and collective Becoming.

Analytical psychology is the system of thought and therapeutic practice developed by the Swiss psychiatrist, Carl G. Jung, Sigmund Freud's pupil and protégé. The psychological terms used in this book, such as *ego, Shadow, active imagination, persona, collective unconscious, Self, projection* and *archetype* were, in the main, developed by Dr. Jung, and I am deeply indebted to this great and courageous innovator for them.

1.

The Archetypes

Living energies that contain ideas and information, specific patterns of instinctual behaviour and thought, are called archetypes. They are the forces that make up the collective unconscious or impersonal part of humanity's psyche that all of us share. These archetypes *automatically* project themselves *outwardly* from within us onto whatever 'screens' are available. The man one dislikes instantly, 'love-at-first-sight', a fondness or antipathy for dogs or cats, a peace-inducing picture of Buddha or some favoured guru, the *Playboy* centrefold, the 'hippie', the frocked priest, *Whistler's Mother* – each of these images acts as a screen for forces that live in all of us, and each of these draws the energies to itself which fit it. Powered by the Light within us, some unknown central Sun, these energies are living intelligent forces within each and all of us which have particular life functions and which weave the fabric that we regard as our personal realities. They are the energies which somehow attach themselves, without our conscious awareness, to everything we meet in the world we call real. Attaching themselves to inanimate objects, the archetypal energies infuse them with positive or negative 'meaning'. Attaching themselves or projecting onto living entities, they both influence the behaviour of those entities and draw back onto themselves a corresponding projection, *always* functioning as a two-way street – therefore, 'If I'm projecting on you, then you're projecting on me.'

These archetypes are the life energies that pour out of each of us unceasingly *night and day, asleep and awake*, influencing everyone in our lives and causing us to be influenced in return. they mould and change our behaviour, our very life structures, but remain invisible to our normal ego consciousness, almost

'The unconscious is both a storehouse and a centre of creation, a place of secrets and hidden things, of joy and terror' (engraving by Gustave Doré from Milton's *Paradise Lost*).

always functioning beneath the level of our awareness. In each human being they constellate in an individual and unique pattern. They form the 'Machinery of the Universe', shaping and reshaping our realities. They are the energies that cause change and fluctuation in our affairs and relationships. These processes are unknown to each of our personal egos, that person you see when you look into your mirror and presume that you are, the body-mind being that includes your physical vehicle and how you think about yourself – your persona, and how others define you.

If you have ever seen someone's ego or personality under-going a Jekyll/Hyde transformation when he became drunk or stoned, or seen someone become psychotic or 'freak out' on drugs to the point where he became someone or something else, you have witnessed one or more of the archetypes displacing or taking over the normal ego. In these situations the person becomes flat and two-dimensional in his interest range. The ego loses its balance and stability and sinks into unconsciousness. In schizophrenia, for instance, the usurping archetype in control seeks only its own gratification, and the other inner archetypal energies starve. This is, perhaps, why schizophrenia is usually a deteriorating disease unless the other archetypal forces can be brought back into balance and the ego resurrected and made strong. The inner archetypes must be in balance, each working with the others and with the ego, for harmony and balance to exist in the life.

Once archetypes have projected out onto the screen of an object, situation or person, they resist removal from the screen until their energy has been satisfied. As an extreme example, if the alcoholic can resist that first drink, he may be able to control the archetypal forces; if not, the unleashed power of the unconscious archetype projected into the alcohol controls him. If the first action in any compulsive behaviour chain can be avoided, the acting out of the compulsion may be inhibited, giving more time for the development of new habit patterns and transformation of the compulsion into behaviour more useful to the individual.

In ancient Egypt the archetypes were called *neters* and were understood with a depth and sophistication that makes our current understanding seem naive. Isha Schwaller de Lubicz speaks of them in her two books: *Her-Bak, 'Chick Pea,' The Living Face of Ancient Egypt* and *Her-Bak, Egyptian Initiate*. (Throughout the following quotations I have substituted 'archetypes' for *'neters'* to avoid confusion.)

'The archetypes are the casual Powers— primary causes and secondary causes – of everything that manifests itself in the Universe; they are the principles, agents and functions of these manifestations.'[1]

They are 'Ideas immanent or virtually contained in nature which give substance form throughout the phases of continuous creation and all genesis.'

'The archetypes are the functional principles of nature . . . Our sense and cerebral intelligence can't grasp them in the abstract; but sense and cerebral intelligence can study the evidence of their essential quality throughout the scale of creatures . . . Power originates action . . . It is therefore immanent in the archetype-nature. But it comprises two elements, natural force and its potential, which can be modified by other archetype-powers and conditioned by the creature, thing or situation in which it is active.'

'But it is difficult for human intelligence to grasp the idea of unity in the creative source and the multiplicity evident in nature. The archetypes are spiritual powers, qualities of divine Force, potentially all that will appear, work, develop in creatures. They are states of a consciousness which is not to be confused with the consciousness that results from existence. Their consciousness is a quality that enters into relations with things in a character that is invariable and doesn't change, as for example the quality 'warmth', whereas the creature changes constantly in the growth of its consciousness, which is the road to liberation from its corporal state.'

'We know that archetype is before man, idea before thing. We know that the same function, in the same circumstances, will give similar results: it is sensible to note the characters of function and circumstances that produced such and such a phenomenon. Isn't an archetype a manifest quality? One ascends from nature to archetype, through whose symbols one may get "to know nature".'

'An archetype is a principle or an agent of a cosmic law or function. It acts and manifests itself by virtue of its own determinism, which is a law of "necessity" independent of the subjects that submit to it. An archetype acts according to its function whether it is unknown or known to human beings; it is indifferent to the names that are attributed to it.'

'In order to understand the meaning of the archetypes, they must be regarded . . . in their own domain of action, nature. We have nature incessantly before us, imposing her laws upon us and *manifesting* the development of a being through all its transformations. Whatever . . . names are given to the forces that rule nature, they always relate to principles that can be known through their effects – that is, through natural phenomena. These principles are the archetypes, and the phenomena are the manifested effects of archetypes, or cosmic functions.'

'When a man has liberated his (personal) archetype (the Self), he becomes an "emitter". . . and does the work of "those who are in their caves". That is, he shares the work of cosmic powers with the acquired consciousness of cosmic Man.'

'We must note . . . what differentiates archetypes from human beings relative to the microcosm: An archetype is not the microcosm, but an aspect or a principal function of it. A human being is the microcosm; he synthesizes the archetypes.'

'Going deeply into Egyptian theology, beyond the three principles of creator, animator, and redeemer and the universal feminine principle, one finds that *the archetypes are of nature* – by "nature" is meant all states that are transitory and relative in relation to the eternal state of the spirit of origin and to the spiritual consciousness acquired throughout nature.'[2]

Hence the archetypes are those energies which create and sustain our personal realities – aspects of God, if you will, that are experientially available to each and all of us.

[1]Isha Schwaller de Lubicz, *Her-Bak, 'Chick-Pea', the Living Face of Ancient Egypt* (New York: Inner Traditions International, Ltd., 1978), p.340.

[2]Isha Schwaller de Lubicz, *Her-Bak, Egyptian Initiate* (New York: Inner Traditions International, Ltd., 1978), p.61, 90, 148-149, 157, 225, 310, 324, 326.

2.

The Tarot

The tarot cards are the most easily obtainable set of picture/symbols of archetypal energies available to Westerners. The tarot is a deck of 78 cards which is divided into two sections: the Major Arcana or Trumps consisting of the 22 main images, and the Minor Arcana containing the remaining 56 cards. These cards of unknown origin appeared in Europe around the end of the 13th Century. They are the ancestors of our modern playing cards. The Major Arcana contain images of 22 universal archetypal forces. These are named *The Fool, The Magician, The High Priestess, The Empress* or *Queen, The King* or *Emperor, The High Priest* or *Hierophant, The Lovers* or *Twins, The Chariot, Strength, The Hermit, The Wheel of Fortune, Justice, The Hanged Man, Death, Temperance, Old Pan* or *The Devil, The Lightning-Struck Tower, The Star, The Moon, The Sun, The Last Judgement* or *Resurrection* and *The World.* They relate astrologically to the twelve signs of the zodiac, the eight planets (excluding Earth), the sun and the moon. (It is interesting to note that the architects of the tarot provided images or slots for Uranus, Neptune and Pluto, although these planets were not discovered until more than 400 years after the tarot's initial appearance, Uranus being discovered in 1781, Neptune in 1846 and Pluto in 1930.)

In his *Archetypes of the Collective Unconscious* Carl Jung refers to the pictures of the tarot as being descended from trans-formation archetypes. These 22 symbolic pictures are images of archetypal energies which project out of each of us and establish and sustain the reality we perceive around ourselves – the form of each individual world, its characters, and the human relationships we experience. (This is most apparent to anyone versed in the art and science of astrology.)

Eleven Tarot trumps from the French 'Charles VI' deck (c. 1390).

These archetypal energies exist in what physics and brain science refer to as a *primary frequency realm*. Karl Pribram, the neuroscientist from Stanford University in California, theorizes a 'primary reality' which is a 'frequency domain', an 'invisible matrix' that produces the universe as a hologram. The 22 archetypal energy forms pictured in tarot are the specific energies that come from this primary frequency realm within each of us and create and sustain the holographic universe we individually and collectively perceive.

3.

Astrology

A natal horoscope calculated for the month, day, year and exact minute of an individual's birth at the exact latitude and longitude of the birthplace gives the film plot or blueprint of that individual's life experience or 'movie' – the world, both inner and outer, through that specific individual's eyes. Over the days and months and years, the inner cycles that correspond to the planets' movements in the heavens activate elements in that individual blueprint, causing the movie to live itself out. Not only can a competent astrologer recount *that* particular individual's life events from the individual's natal horoscope; he can also describe what is taking place or has taken place in the lives of *everyone that particular person is related to* through blood, law or role relationship. For example, the astrologer can tell of the individual's eldest sister's current marriage crisis, dates of recent chaos or luck in the person's own love area, of his third child's difficulties at school, of the erratic behaviour of his employer – all from *the individual's own natal pattern*, without knowledge of any of the other people's lives or birth patterns. He can describe the personalities and physical characteristics of the parents and of aunts, uncles and distant relatives the individual hasn't seen since childhood and has all but forgotten. The astrologer can tell of troubled areas in the lives of second and third cousins in remote parts of the world – again, all from the individual's own horoscopic pattern.

That a stranger, the astrologer, is able to deliver this sort of accurate personal information illustrates that some sort of machinery is at work in which the individual himself is the major cog. When the astrologer gives him intimate life details and concise dates, past and present, about anyone in his family after whom he chooses to inquire, an individual knows that

'The Astrologer' (engraving by S. Lucas).

more than coincidence is involved. It is only from *his* horoscope that the astrologer obtains the information, not the horoscopes of his relatives.

How is he connected to brother Joe's broken leg? What is his relation to sister Jan's religious conversion? Is *he* to blame for the 'bad' things that occur that are described in his horoscope? Is he to be credited with the 'good'? And if he *is* somehow connected to all these events and people, as the astrologer will have demonstrated, can *he* make things better for all concerned?

4.

Projection

Let us return to the 22 archetypal forces that the tarot images present. These forces or energies are projecting out from each of us all of the time, establishing the realities we find ourselves experiencing. If one of them is repressed, pushed away from the level of ego consciousness into the dark depths of the psyche, it is rendered 'negative' or 'evil' to our ego judgement, and it functions as a negative hook or magnet for experience in our outer worlds, drawing to us or to our 'parts' (those to whom we are related in some way) the very quality we had attempted to avoid through the repression process.

If one considers them as the pure energy which they are, none of the archetypal forces is or can be essentially 'good' or 'evil'. They are *neutral*, but potent, energies capable of presenting themselves as either. It is their degree of repression or suppression, if any, that makes them appear as 'good' or 'bad', 'positive' or 'negative', 'plus' or 'minus', as they project out into our lives, creating and sustaining the realities we experience. The level at which they exist in us in relation to their assimilation or non-assimilation by our egos – whether accepted or rejected, expressed or unexpressed, nourished or starved – determines how we judge the manifestations and situations they create as projections out in reality. Change the ego relationship to the archetypal force within yourself and you change the projected 'screen' as it exists in your outer world. What we label 'evil' or 'bad' are those forces within ourselves that we have pushed into unconsciousness, have never attempted to assimilate into our consciousness, and are unconscious of, acting on those receptive or needful screens in our environments. 'Evil' is unconsciousness of repressed energy, and those who are concerned about its prevalence in

80. XVI. ♂

THE TOWER

Trump of *The Tower* from Jerry Kay's *Book of Thoth* Tarot Deck.

their worlds would do well to seek the source of that 'evil' within themselves. 'Evil' results from ignorance of the way the multi-dimensional laws of the Universe work.

Here is an astrological example. The planet Mars (called *The Lightning-Struck Tower* in tarot) has to do with our instinctual animal energies. It signifies much sexual force and aggressive life 'go' energy. If it is *suppressed*, that is, the forces symbolized by this planet are suppressed, the usual manifestation in us will be irritability or anger, temper or 'pushiness'. If Mars exists as a *repressed* force within (for example, if it is located in the 12th section or *House* of a horoscope where those forces *which we are born with as repressed factors* reside), it can act as a negative magnet in our realities and draw extreme anger or violence down upon us or cause health or work traumas in our partners' lives without any ego awareness of participation in or connection to those traumas.

Jesus taught, 'The Kingdom of Heaven is within you'. However, we keep looking everywhere but within for our solutions and our peace. The process of receiving from within is the major key to expanding consciousness, but we are conditioned from childhood to look without. Our parents, our teachers and our peers dismiss the inner worlds with such typical responses as: 'It's only your imagination', or 'Be realistic – quit dreaming', or 'You're just putting yourself on'. The 'imaginary playmate' of the sensitive child is discouraged, ignored or 'trained' out, causing the child to lose his key to the inner worlds, perhaps, forever. How many of our Christian evangelists or gurus or rabbis or priests encourage this individual quest within, this inner search for the Kingdom of Heaven, a quest that might weaken or remove the authority of their own personal 'king'-dom? Everyone is encouraged to go on someone else's trip, understand and believe through another's experiences or dogma – few are encouraged to embark on their own inner journey. Everyone tends to look for his teacher or guru in the outer world – few look within where he exists.

Projection is the unconscious phenomenon which acts to transmit our inner archetypes onto the available screens or receivers in our outer worlds. This can be most easily noted in those people or things one actively and knowingly dislikes or hates. Whatever is threatening or uncomfortable to the current ego, generally becomes suppressed or repressed –

pushed down into the darkness within us where we become unaware of it. But this process does not get rid of the problem. Instead, the repression, which is an expenditure of directional psychic energy (down, away from the ego, away from the light of consciousness into the darkness of unconsciousness), acts as a magnet that draws from the outer world those very qualities our egos have rejected, because the force being pushed away will have its literal expression in some way. Since some kind of outer screen is always available to us, projection takes place – the outer screen presenting the hook or passive psychic structure to which the 'hang-up' or unconscious material attaches itself by the mechanism or projection. The receiver fills with the qualities and energies of the repressed or suppressed material causing our egos to react with 'hate' or 'dislike'.

Some projections are considered 'good' or desirable by the social norms or current standards of the collective unconscious which condition the values and beliefs that our egos hold. Falling in love, as opposed to loving, is one of the most prevalent forms of 'positive' projection in human society. It is Nature's tool that brings couples together to perpetuate the species. When we 'fall in love', we experience the projection of some *ideal* archetypal part of ourselves onto the screen of another person who serves as a receiver for that ideal. The archetype carries with it and imposes on the 'loved one' a whole range of potential desires, behaviour patterns, emotional responses and psychological 'sets', all encouraged and nourished by the behaviour and psychological expectations of the person projecting the archetype. 'Falling in love' is literally loving a part of oneself which the projection process places on the physical and psychological being of another. This displacement and reception of a part of one's being causes the bliss of love, if the other willingly receives and responds to it, or the pain of love, if the other rejects or only partially accepts the projection. 'Falling in love' makes demands on the other, willing or unwilling. 'Loving' is free and giving; it requires nothing in return, has no expectation, accepts the other without judgement or reservation, and wants only that which can be freely and willingly given out of the other's Self. The relationships where 'falling in love' turns into 'loving' as the initial projection wanes are those that endure with the greatest depth and beauty.

Projection sends component energies of the Self out into the world. When these energies remain unconscious, the result is loss of an individual's psychic energy and freedom. When the energies are made conscious (with ego and Self being brought into balance with the ego serving and acting as vehicle for the Self), the result is a free individual who radiates light and love into the world around him. In contrast, when two individuals are involved in a deeply repressed projection, both experience a curtailment of the freedom of their individual egos and a subsequent energy loss. You can be sure that you are involved in a deep-seated unconscious projection with those individuals whose mere physical presence exhausts you for no reason you can find. Most often this 'exhaustion relationship' can be found with a member of one's immediate family, often the mother. Experiment the next time you encounter this individual. Don't *expect* the old responses and behaviour. Let the person be *new*, and send love out of your heart *consciously*. Love is the greatest freeing energy we have. You may be surprised at the results for you both.

Figure 1 below is a diagram of the mechanics of the process of projection. Let us call **A** the blueprint or 'set film strip' of an individual: in astrology this would be the **natal pattern** or natal horoscope of the person. Let **B** represent the ego structure which is being constantly shifted and modified by the forces activating it from **A**: this **B** in astrology would be the Rising Sign or Ascendant of a horoscope. Together **A** and **B** constitute the moving film or inherent flowing pattern of a life. As long as the source energy, **C**, flows unconsciously

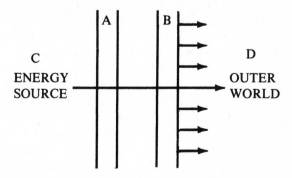

Figure 1: Diagram of the mechanics of the process of projection.

along our nerve channels from within to without through this film, *free will remains an ego illusion*. But when, through meditation, the ego attempts to move along these same flow channels *back* toward its own source or centre, **C** in the diagram, an assimilation and consciousness of these source-energies begins, and one can begin to make real choices and become truly free. Freedom is *impossible* so long as we think of **D**, the outer world and its elements, as the source or basis of our realities. It is only when we learn that the foundation of our realities lies within that we find ourselves on the road to individual freedom and consciousness, no longer able to take the role of victim of circumstances. How long have we heard of the 'Kingdom within' without really understanding what this means? **Free will is not a 'given'.** It must be earned, and the price of consciousness and free will is the death and rebirth of the current ego.

You *yourself* hold the unique key to your own self development and spiritual evolution. No one outside of you holds that key. To change anything in your personal reality effectively or permanently, you must seek the cause of its current reality manifestation at its source or point of origin, or as close to that point as you are able to, within yourself. As long as unconscious projection is taking place, everyone in your outer world is *literally* some part of yourself projecting and functioning as the perceived ego of the other – *all* are actors in *your* movie taking their positive and negative roles to fit *your* particular movie script. Your current ego (what you presently consider yourself to be) acts as a membrane between the forces flowing out of you onto your world and the forces flowing back onto and into you from the other projecting entities in your personal reality. Until you can **experience** how your projecting energies are affecting others, you will *never* understand how their projections are affecting you in turn.

Assume for a moment that the unconscious contains various adjacent levels. Let us say that there are four of these levels, each containing a greater degree of darkness or unconsciousness as they exist in a progressive relationship *away* from the awareness of the ego. In these four successive levels of the unconscious live all the energies that give us life, that create and sustain our experienced realities. Here lie our psychic capabilities, the body's abilities to maintain and repair itself, the monitor of breathing and heart action, our forgotten

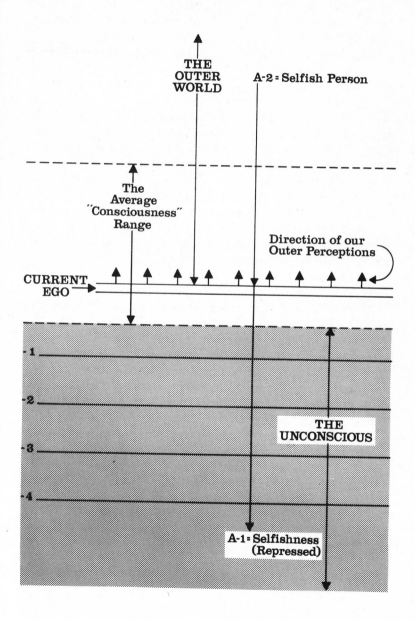

Figure 2: Graph illustrating the repression of an energy constellation (graphics by Karl T. Tani).

memories, our latent dreams, the central Sun or Source we each carry – all that we are unaware of. The unconscious is both a storehouse and a centre of creation, a place of secrets and hidden things, of joy and terror.

Figure 2 is an example of the projection process illustrating a repression of an energy constellation, the quality called Selfishness (A-1 in the diagram), into the darkness of the unconscious. Let us say that an individual has this quality repressed within at the level called Minus 4 in the diagram, the level furthest from ego awareness where the deepest repressions dwell. A *directional* expenditure of psychic energy is required to keep it pushed to this depth, away from any ego awareness. A *balancing component* of some sort from the outer world is required to stabilize the negative energy at the depth of unconsciousness. The psychic radar which exists in all of us searches our environments and draws to us from the outer world, A-2, the person or persons who have the need to live out this quality of Selfishness unconsciously and will accept the projection of this energy constellation from us because of their corresponding unconsciousness.

All of our repressed or suppressed energies take on the qualities of the levels of darkness in which they exist. The qualities of the level of unconsciousness in which they live within us determine how they manifest out in our worlds. Push your own creative energies away from your ego awareness, and you will draw to you creative people who will live those energies out for you. Push your hates into the darkness, and you will draw the hateful into your world so that those energies can have their expressions. All that we brand 'bad' or 'evil' in our worlds act as mirrors of our own unconsciousness. Jesus' advice to 'Love thine enemies' is good contemporary advice, for nothing heals and brings forth our negative parts transformed, within and without, as does the power of love.

5.

Active Imagination

Active imagination, an ancient metaphysical meditation tool rediscovered by Dr Jung just before the beginning of World War I, is the primary process or method utilized in the Inner Guide Meditation. In his discussions of alchemy Jung compares the process of active imagination to the production of the Philosopher's Stone of the Alchemists. He describes the process in *Mysterium Coniunctionis:* 'Its purpose was to create, in the form of a substance, that 'truth', the celestial balsam or life principle, which is identical with the God-image. Psychologically, it was a representation of the individuation process by means of chemical substances and procedures, or what we today call active imagination. This is a method which is used spontaneously by nature herself or can be taught... As a rule it occurs when the analysis has constellated the opposites so powerfully that a union or synthesis of the personality becomes an imperative necessity. Such a situation is bound to arise when the analysis of the psychic contents, of the patient's attitude and particularly of his dreams, has brought the compensatory or complementary images from the unconscious so insistently before his mind that the conflict between the conscious and the unconscious personality becomes open and critical. When this confrontation is confined to partial aspects of the unconscious the conflict is limited and the solution simple: the patient, with insight and some resignation or a feeling of resentment, places himself on the side of reason and convention. Though the unconscious motifs are repressed again, as before, the unconscious is satisfied to a certain extent, because the patient must now make a conscious effort to live according to its principles and, in addition, is constantly reminded of the existence of the

repressed by annoying resentments. But if his recognition of
the shadow is as complete as he can make it, then conflict and
disorientation ensue, an equally strong Yes and No which he
can no longer keep apart by a rational decision. He cannot
transform his clinical neurosis into the less conspicuous
neurosis of cynicism; in other words, he can no longer hide the
conflict behind a mask. It requires a real solution and
necessitates a third thing in which the opposition can unite.
Here the logic of the intellect usually fails, for in a logical
antithesis there is no third. The 'solvent' can only be of an
irrational nature. In nature the resolution of opposites is
always an energic process: she acts *symbolically* in the truest
sense of the word, doing something that expresses both sides,
just as a waterfall visibly mediates between above and below.
The waterfall itself is then the incommensurable third. In an
open and unresolved conflict dreams and fantasies occur
which, like the waterfall, illustrate the tension and nature of
the opposites, and thus prepare the synthesis.

'This process can, as I have said, take place spontaneously
or be artificially induced. In the latter case you choose a
dream, or some other fantasy-image, and concentrate on it by
simply catching hold of it and looking at it. You can also use a
bad mood as a starting-point, and then try to find out what sort
of fantasy-image it will produce, or what image expresses this
mood. You then fix this image in the mind by concentrating
your attention. Usually it will alter, as the mere fact of
contemplating it animates it. The alterations must be carefully
noted down all the time, for they reflect the psychic processes
in the unconscious background, which appear in the form of
images consisting of conscious memory material. In this way
conscious and unconscious are united, just as a waterfall
connects above and below. A chain of fantasy ideas develops
and gradually takes on a dramatic character: the passive
process becomes an action. At first it consists of projected
figures, and these images are observed like scenes in the
theatre... As a rule there is a marked tendency simply to enjoy
this interior entertainment and to leave it at that. Then, of
course, there is no real progress but only endless variations on
the same theme, which is not the point of the exercise at all.
What is enacted on the stage still remains a background
process; it does not move the observer in any way, and the less
it moves him the smaller will be the cathartic effect of this

private theatre. The piece that is being played does not want merely to be watched impartially, it wants to compel his participation. If the observer understands that his own drama is being performed on this inner stage, he cannot remain indifferent to the plot and its dénouement. He will notice, as the actors appear one by one and the plot thickens, that they all have some purposeful relationship to his conscious situation, that he is being addressed by the unconscious, and that it causes these fantasy-images to appear before him. He therefore feels compelled, or is encouraged . . . to take part in the play and, instead of just sitting in a theatre, really have it out with his alter ego. For nothing in us ever remains quite uncontradicted, and consciousness can take up no position which will not call up, somewhere in the dark corners of the psyche, a negation or a compensatory effect, approval or resentment. This process of coming to terms with the Other (the other half or Shadow side of ourselves) in us is well worthwhile, because in this way we get to know aspects of our natures which we would not allow anybody else to show us and which we ourselves would never have admitted. It is very important to fix this whole procedure in writing at the time of its occurrence, for you then have ocular evidence that will effectively counteract the ever-ready tendency to self-deception. A running commentary is absolutely necessary in dealing with the shadow, because otherwise its actuality cannot be fixed. Only in this . . . way is it possible to gain a positive insight into the complex nature of one's own personality'.[1]

Here Jung outlines the technique of active imagination, though he presents it within the structure of an analytical relationship between doctor and patient. The technique is a process of interacting with and gradually assimilating, as a result of these interactions, those parts of ourselves that our current egos are ignorant of or have only partially assimilated. It is an invaluable experiential process, and in the Inner Guide Meditation it brings back to the Guide that energy and wisdom which up to now we have been conditioned to project out from within onto analyst, priest or guru.

[1]Carl G. Jung, *Mysterium Coniunctionis*, ed. H. Read, M. Fordham, G. Adler, trans. R. F. C. Hull, *The Collected Works of C. G. Jung*, Bollingen Series XX, vol. 14 (Princeton: Princeton University Press, 1963), p.495-496.

'The Guide and I into that hidden road now entered, to return to the bright world' (engraving by Gustave Doré from Dante's *Inferno*).

6.

Plato's Allegory of the Cave

'Imagine the condition of men living in a sort of cavernous chamber underground, with an entrance open to the light and a long passage all down the cave. Here they have been from childhood, chained by the leg and also by the neck, so that they cannot move and can see only what is in front of them, because the chains will not let them turn their heads. At some distance higher up is the light of a fire burning behind them; and between the prisoners and the fire is a track with a parapet built along it, like the screen at a puppet-show, which hides the performers while they show their puppets over the top.

'Now behind this parapet imagine persons carrying along various artificial objects, including figures of men and animals in wood or stone or other materials, which project above the parapet. Naturally, some of these persons will be talking, others silent.'

'It is a strange picture,' he said, 'and a strange sort of prisoners.'

'Like ourselves,' I (Socrates) replied; 'for in the first place prisoners so confined would have seen nothing of themselves or of one another, except the shadows thrown by the fire-light on the wall of the cave facing them, would they?'

'Not if all their lives they had been prevented from moving their heads.'

'And they would have seen as little of the objects carried past.'

'Of course.'

'Now, if they could talk to one another, would they not suppose that their words referred only to those passing shadows which they saw?'

'Necessarily.'

'And suppose their prison had an echo from the wall facing them? When one of the people crossing behind them spoke, they could only suppose that the sound came from the shadow passing before their eyes.'

'No doubt.'

'In every way, then, such prisoners would recognize as reality nothing but the shadows of those artificial objects.'

'Inevitably.'

'Now consider what would happen if their release from the chains and the healing of their unwisdom should come about in this way. Suppose one of them was set free and forced suddenly to stand up, turn his head, and walk with eyes lifted in the light; all these movements would be painful, and he would be too dazzled to make out the objects whose shadows he had been used to seeing. What do you think he would say, if someone told him what he had formerly seen was meaningless illusion, but now, being somewhat nearer to reality and turned towards more real objects, he was getting a truer view? Suppose further that he were shown then various objects being carried by and were made to say, in reply to questions, what each of them was. Would he not be perplexed and believe the objects now shown to him to be not so real as what he formerly saw?'

'Yes, not nearly so real.'

'And if he were forced to look at the fire-light itself, would not his eyes ache, so that he would try to escape and turn back to the things which he could see distinctly, convinced that they really were clearer to him than these other objects now being shown to him?'

'Yes.'

'And suppose someone were to drag him away forcibly up the steep and rugged ascent and not let him go until he had hauled him out into the sunlight, would he not suffer pain and vexation at such treatment, and, when he had come out into the light, find his eyes so full of its radiance that he could not see a single one of the things that he was now told were real?'

'Certainly he would not see them all at once.'

'He would need, then, to grow accustomed before he could see things in that upper world. At first it would be easiest to make out shadows, and then the images of men and things reflected in Homer's Achilles, that he would far sooner "be on earth as a hired servant in the house of a landless man"

(Achilles' statement in Hades) or endure anything rather than go back to his old beliefs and live in the old way?'

'Yes, he would prefer any fate to such a life.'

'Now imagine what would happen if he went down again to take his former seat in the cave. Coming suddenly out of the sunlight, his eyes would be filled with darkness. He might be required once more to deliver his opinion on those shadows, in competition with the prisoners who had never been released, while his eyesight was still dim and unsteady; and it might take some time to become used to the darkness. They would laugh at him and say that he had gone up only to come back with his sight ruined; it was worth no one's while even to attempt the ascent. If they could lay hands on the man who was trying to set them free and lead them up, they would kill him.'

'Yes, they would.'[1]

Here Socrates speaking to Glaucon illustrates aspects of the process of projection. What we perceive in our outer realities are but shadows cast by images within, made visible by some unknown Light within or central Sun. 'It's all in your head, y'know,' said one of the Beatles. Perhaps not exactly in our heads, but somewhere within us or through the doors of ourselves lie the sources that present these animated shadows to us, that project on the world through a kind of holographic film strip each of us possesses or is. Also, we each have an inner liberator, who will release us from our chains, and who will teach us to recognize those shadow- making images as he leads us toward the realization of our own Source, taking care that our inner eye not be blinded, while helping us become gradually more accustomed to image and light as he moves us toward that Source.

'Shadow' pictures of Jesus and the Virgin on an old woman's living room wall seem to speak to her, giving her advice on her life affairs, consoling her in her griefs. A 'shadow' Venus in a Botticelli *Birth of Venus* art print on a young man's bedroom wall presents an echo, whispering of the delight of womanhood and promising life's pleasures. A 'shadow' masquerading as a shopkeeper's first dollar bill, framed and mounted above the shop counter, tells him of money to come, of stability, of business growth. A 'shadow' presenting itself as a portrait of Satan echoes commands and secrets of power to the 'black magician'.

These are all shadows in the exact sense that Plato speaks of them, but each individual will swear to their reality. All feel the source of the communication to be the image they can see or touch. Each will argue for the validity of his particular 'shadow' on the wall of his own 'cave'.

Just as a motion picture projector projects its images upon a screen, these shadows on which the individuals focus merely serve as screens for living forces being drawn or projected out from each of the people. From the old woman the 'shadow images' of Jesus and Mary draw energies dealing with love and motherhood. Out of the young man, a force or energy having to do with the pleasure principle and physical love is pulled. The shopkeeper projects an organic growth force, and, the black magician, a force dealing with power and paranoia. None is aware of the inner sources that the 'shadow images' are drawing from and focusing upon the outer images or forms. The intelligence, the information seem to dwell in the image, to come from it, separate and distinct from the individual involved.

[1] Plato *The Republic* trans. F. M. Cornford (New York: Oxford University Press, 1945), pp.227-231.

7.

The Initial Experiments

The experience of the archetype is frequently guarded as the closest personal secret, because it is felt to strike into the very core of one's being . . . (These experiences) demand to be individually shaped in and by each man's life and work. They are images sprung from the life, the joys and sorrows, of our ancestors; and to live they seek to return, not in experience only, but in deed. Because of their opposition to the conscious mind they cannot be translated straight into our world; hence a way must be found that can mediate between conscious and unconscious reality.[1]

Carl G. Jung

In 1969 I was in Jungian analysis with an analytical psychologist in Los Angeles, California. It was going slowly, as analysis usually does. The analyst went off to Zurich on some business, and I was left with the forward-impelling inertia of someone whose unconscious has been activated.

I had been using the 'active imagination' technique in my analytic sessions through my own insistence, going back to dreams and finishing or re-working them. I was fascinated by the living experiences I had while exploring my psyche. The analyst had emphasized the dangers of the active imagination process – of repressed unconscious forces that might overcome the ego and usurp it, of the terror that an encounter with repressed energy forms could trigger. But fire is a fascination to the unburned.

In the analyst's absence I was experimenting with astrological and tarot imagery (I was an astrologer by profession at that time), attempting to puzzle out the psychological 'physics' involved in getting information from the tarot cards as one read them spread on a table before himself. I deduced that the accurate data I was able to obtain from these readings had to have their origins somewhere deep within my psyche. If, say, the Tarot *High Priestess* card could 'tell' me of events happening in a distant city by projecting an energy force with this particular information from within me out onto a card screen, then how much more accurately could 'she', the archetypal force of *The High Priestess*, communicate with me face to face in the inner world through the process of active imagination.

I had also at the time just finished reading Richard Wilhelm's translation of the Chinese classic, *The Secret of the Golden Flower*, in which the secret seemed to be to 'circulate the light backwards', or, as I interpreted it, to force the mental energy back along the same channels or nerve pathways that the projection energy flowed out on.

I attempted to do this by inventing a staircase in my imagination that would take me within to those archetypal images I was seeking. And it worked! I reached a room at the bottom of my stairway, thought of *The High Priestess*, and she was *there*, a *living* presence in that inner world, different from the picture on the tarot card, but without a doubt *The High Priestess* as a reality within me. And the experience seemed to be happening *there*, in some other plane or reality, totally unconnected with the *here* of the normally experienced outer world.

I was delighted with my new toy. It had a reality and a freshness I hadn't experienced since childhood, and there was no doubt about the experiential realness of it. I was with the Tarot *Sun*, and my body became warm and relaxed. *The Magician* taught me things I had never heard of in my outer reality. The presence of the Tarot *Fool* would cause a pins and needles sensation in my limbs.

But then I had an experience that acutely demonstrated the analyst's warnings about the dangers of active imagination as it is practiced in analytical psychology. I was inside the room where I came into contact with the archetypal forms when an image of the Tarot *Old Pan* or *Devil* appeared, unsummoned and unwanted. It was a classic Christian devil with an emanation of 'evil' as real as the beneficence I had felt when interacting with the archetype of *The Sun*. I tried to end the experience by opening my eyes, but I discovered that I was unable to move or perform this simple feat. I was paralyzed. I began to panic. I seemed to be frozen in the chair. *The Old Pan* entity became even more menacing than before, placing himself in my inner world between me and the stairway to the outer world and safety. The panic finally subsided (although not the fear), and I further tried to manoeuvre to the stairway around the figure, but to no avail. This entity of the inner world blocked my every move whenever I attempted the stairs. He did not advance toward me but remained as a moving barrier to any possible exit. It even crossed my mind that I might be discovered by the outer world in this catatonic state and be taken off to the nearest psychiatric hospital. I couldn't even call out to try to communicate my situation to anyone who might be within hearing.

Finally, I was able to calm myself and concentrate on my outer body sufficiently to try to move a finger on my right hand. Using all my will and ignoring the *Old Pan* figure entirely, I managed this feat, and it broke the state in which I had been locked. The experience was so frightening, however, that I decided then and there never again to attempt another venture into the realms of the unconscious without the presence of a trained analyst.

A few months passed. Fear weakened with this passage of time, and curiosity increased. There *had* to be some safe way to go back 'down there' without having to be dependent on an analyst's presence. It was so like a foreign country whose laws and customs I did not know. This analogy triggered the thought that perhaps 'guides' existed there as they do in other foreign countries, their roles being created in response to travellers' needs. Throughout the myths, poetry, fairy tales and spiritual literature of the world, guides in some form have been spoken of or referred to – the spirit guides of trance mediums, the 'still, small voice within', Dante's Virgil, Alice's White Rabbit, the Guides mentioned in the writings of Agni Yoga, the Guardians of the Pueblo Indians of North America. Perhaps if I attempted the descent once more –

All proceeded as before: I found my inner stairway and cautiously descended. I reached the bottom. The room was deserted. Standing close to the stairs, I called out for a guide to appear. At first nothing happened, but then a feeling of love and warmth touched me from my left. Slowly I moved away from the staircase through an opening that I now noticed on the left. I passed through the opening, and, to the right of it, I saw an old man standing. He was dressed in striped robes of muted colours, had whiskers, was of medium height and wore a turban. Kindness and gentleness radiated from him. I asked if he were a 'guide'. He responded that he was *my* Inner Guide and that his name was 'Aman'. I told him of my terrifying experience with the Tarot *Old Pan* energy, and he explained that it was my fear that had made the experience so potentially dangerous. I asked him if he could truly guide and teach me in this strange, beautiful and frightening inner world and if he could protect me from such experiences as I had had with *Old Pan*. He stated simply that he always *had* tried to guide and protect me and always would if I requested and allowed him to do so. And so began the inner adventure and the beginnings of true choice and freedom in my life.

I was at this time a conventional astrologer, delineating horoscopes for those who were referred to me, who often were also working in Jungian analysis, but this became increasingly frustrating for me. It was like telling someone about the *trap* he had been born into without being able to give him any key for transcending it except a new rationalization process and the new vocabulary of astrology.

It was during this same time period that I was also experimenting with the tarot cards. It occurred to me that, as the 22 tarot images correspond to the primary astrological factors (12 zodiacal signs, 8 planets, the sun and the moon), the entire horoscope or solar system birth pattern might be re-translated and expressed in terms of these tarot forms. Perhaps one could resolve the energy conflicts described in the horoscope by *arbitrating* the 'quarrels' ('hard angles' and polarizations) between the archetypal energies in the inner world, by allowing antagonistic energy systems to begin touching each other and restructuring their relationships and energy flows.

I did this re-translation with my own horoscope as the base. Where the planet Uranus was in a 90° relationship or 'hard angle' to the planet Saturn, I interpreted it as *The Fool* (Uranus) and *The World* (Saturn) being antagonistic. Where Saturn was in an 180° relationship or *opposition* aspect to the planet Pluto, I transposed it to *The World* (Saturn) and *The Last Judgement* (Pluto) being polarized, and so on with all the so-called 'afflictions' or 'hard angles' in my natal pattern. I then attempted the arbitrations.

Tarot trump *Death* from the D.O.M.E. Meditation Cards by Sheila W. Ross.

Trump of *Old Pan* based on the Jerry Kay *Book of Thoth* Tarot Deck.

Trump of *The World* based on the B.O.T.A. Tarot Deck.

Trump of *The Wheel of Fortune* from the Lama Foundation Tarot Deck, 1969.

'Never go into the inner world without your Inner Guide'
(engraving by Gustave Doré from Dante's *Inferno*).

It was during this initial arbitration phase that I experienced the difference between *ego* and *non-ego* elements in my own psyche. My imagination took on a life of its own. Conflicting archetypal forms *would not* be pushed into agreement or easy reconciliation. Where I had supposed, 'I'm making most of this up,' I soon found experiences full of surprises. It became dramatically clear to me that these were *living* entities I was dealing with and that my ego could not get them to cooperate or come together just because I thought they should or asked them to. They seemed to be separate, sometimes alien, entities totally unlike any familiar aspect of myself, with likes and dislikes, interests and aversions, moods and temperaments of their own. Their behaviour, as I observed and interacted with them, was often completely unpredictable. Occasionally they were hostile to me. Sometimes they totally ignored my presence, and only with the greatest effort could I attract their attention and get them to communicate with me. To get behaviour change or cooperation from them, *I* usually had to agree to make changes in my outer world, modify my behaviour or agree on new actions or directions. They were most explicit about the changes they required from me or from my life in exchange for their cooperation or assistance.

As this inner process went on, I began to notice new phenomena occuring in my outer world. Those people in my life whom my ego regarded as negative or destructive began to change for the better or go out of my life. It seemed that everyone around me was suddenly beginning to 'get it together' as I continued to do the inner work. Problems that had been with me since childhood began to drop away. There was usually no high drama in this; I would just notice one day that a life-long problem had not occured for a long time, and, as more time passed, there was no recurrence of it. It had just gone away.

It occurred to me that perhaps others could contact their Inner Guides, so I began trying to get others to their Guides at the conclusion of my horoscope readings. At first I had limited success because of my own tentativeness, but then the Guide contacts increased as did my own confidence in demonstrating the meditation. Friends volunteered time to talk out their inner workings to me, and I began to get a concept of the archetypal forces as collective entities.

I also began to receive feedback from others who were

working on their own with their Guides. They were beginning to get the same kinds of positive life changes and experiences that I had noticed, which were often more dramatic than mine. Reports came of physical healings, mended marriages and spiritual breakthroughs. The common thread throughout seemed to be an alteration, often drastic, of the life values, and an active new spiritual force that gave freshness, meaning and depth to the individual life.

After a few years of helping others find their Inner Guides, I received the astrological surprise of my life. I began to notice a remarkable similarity between one aspect of the horoscopes of the individuals I worked with and their descriptions of the Guides they contacted in their inner worlds. I discovered that **the personality and physical appearance of one's initial Inner Guide corresponds to the Ninth House** (or horoscopic section) **of the individual natal pattern** (when Koch Birthplace House Cusps are used, not Placidean). This is traditionally the section called the **House of God and Religion** and the area describing the individual's philosophic and religious views, as well as his own ability to act as a guide or way-shower for others. In addition, 'false' guides, those inner entities who sometimes appear and represent a personification of an individual's rationalization system, were also described in the natal pattern by the Third House or section of the horoscope. That we are so completely programmed, internally as well as externally, came as a shocking revelation. However, this new insight gave the ability to distinguish the true Guide from the false to anyone versed in astrology, and my confidence in the entire meditation increased, making the initial Guide contact easier for me to initiate. It also showed that the horoscope is a literal road map of the inner world's inhabitants, geography and physics and a tool which can be verified by one's own personal unconscious.

The positive reports continued to reach me. Often frightening material, such as I had experienced with the Tarot *Old Pan* archetype, was reported. The presence and advice of the Guide in each case enabled the individual not only to face the unconscious material that the image represented, but also actually to deal with and transform it. Usually the previously threatening or horrifying image was healed and became a comfortable or enjoyable presence. As the archetypal image in the inner world was healed, all that it had projected upon in the outer world simultaneously healed or changed. 'Negative' relatives would surprisingly change their behaviours. Sudden insight would replace persistent misunderstanding. Hates or objects of hate would vanish or change. All the screens that the previously 'good' or 'evil' archetypal energy had projected upon received the new projection and were transformed.

These sudden outer changes initially produced a common reaction in those experiencing them, including myself. It all seemed 'too fast'. A resistance to sitting down and working with the Guide and the archetypes developed and lasted until our egos got used to the outer changes and assimilated them. Each of us had to reconsider his or her beliefs about reality and how it works. For example, if I could sit and meditate in a chair in Santa Fe, New Mexico, working on an archetypal energy within me that corresponds to my oldest brother in my horoscopic pattern, and have that brother go through sudden positive change fifteen hundred miles away at the same time that the archetype that I project on him (according to my astrological theory) changes in my inner world, something is erroneous in the way we've been taught that reality works. Somehow the energies *I* carry are *making* the world I occupy and experience. Not 'I,' the current ego, but 'I' as a totality. The realization also came that if what I see in my outer world is negative or destructive, this archetypal interaction, with the Guide present, is a process by which I can change or heal the outer by searching out and healing that inner part of myself which participates in the particular manifestation of negativity or unconsciousness. No one can do anything harmful or destructive to anyone else unless the inner unconscious projections of *both* parties set them up to do so. There is no one to blame for anything that happens to us. No one is a victim. The *totality* of each person creates the reality that person experiences. The bad trips or 'bummers' an individual experiences are the inescapable results of his own unconsciousness in thought, word and deed.

The inner work changes the outer world, literally and for the better. At this time I began to understand the Inner Guide Meditation as a spiritual tool that Western culture could use for its own healing. It begins as an *action-oriented, result-based* process which can be tested against and verified by experience and by the individual's own natal horoscope symbology, and it progresses according to an individual's developmental needs. It answers specific questions, aims at specific life targets – a Western method of meditation for the West. And it is a meditation which can be used in the midst of life – on the subway or train, while waiting in the car, during the lunch or coffee break, alone in a motel.

Since its discovery in 1969, thousands of people from all walks of life have been initiated by me and by others who follow the horoscopic road map into the Inner Guide Meditation. No 'bad trips' have been reported. The inner world remains a world with its own peculiar dangers, but the presence of the Guide allows these dangers to be dealt with safely and transformed. The Guides restrain us from going faster in our interactions with the internal energies than our egos *(which include our physical bodies)* can handle and absorb, often refusing to take us into certain inner world areas or suggesting that a specific archetypal form be avoided at the first ego request – or perhaps suddenly pulling us away from one of the inner forms in mid-sentence. When things are happening too fast in our inner or outer lives, the Guides may suggest just sitting or talking with them at the inner meeting place or some special calm and peaceful inner world spot rather than approaching and interacting with any of the archetypes. He may give a quieting *mantra* or teach a Centring ritual or exercise. My initial Guide usually had me sit with my feet in a cool forest brook, close my eyes and let my mind quiet during these times in my life.

What happens in the interaction with the archetypal figures is that *the interaction itself,* just the fact of being with or touching one of the archetypal forms, tends to start the assimilation of its energy by the ego so that the archetype's negative-seeming projection ability is lessened. The more you work with one specific archetype in the inner world, the more you will find yourself becoming free and having expanded choice in the area of life which that archetypal energy governs in your particular pattern.

Let's take the Tarot *High Priestess* for an example. The more time you spend with that form in the inner world and the more positively the image presents itself to you as you interact with it, the more you will notice a corresponding change in those individuals who accept and live out your *High Priestess* projection; the nourishers, sustainers, protectors and mother figures in your life. You will notice a new emotional relationship with your own mother which contains greater freedom, love and individuality for each of you.

It's the same with the 21 other tarot archetypal energy forms. A greater amount of friendliness and love in the relationship between you, the current ego, and a particular archetypal part of yourself will correspond with an improvement in your ego's relationships to those who are screens or receptors for that force or principle. 'As above, so below', goes the ancient Hermetic axiom, or, to paraphrase, 'As within, so without'. If you want to know how *you're* doing, **look at the outside world around you.** *That's* how you're doing.

Since discovering the Inner Guides, information about them seems to be everywhere I look. Plato speaks of the 'instructor' or 'liberator' in the cave allegory. Jung found Philemon, a 'guide' of sorts, as he reports in his *Memories, Dreams, Reflections*, but didn't, to my knowledge, develop and incorporate the Guides into his active imagination methods. In the literature of magic, guides are mentioned and used. They appear in the fairy tales and myths of all man's cultures. Everyone knows the concept of the Guardian Angel. The spirit guides mentioned by Spiritualists and others contacting the inner planes seem often to be true Guides. But the physics of *where* they exist seems to have been misunderstood, their existence being projected outside of the person channeling the spirit as often as not. The Inner Guides sometimes show up spontaneously in LSD experiences, as John C. Lilly reports in his *The Center of the Cyclone*, or in other altered states of consciousness experiences, and some children know them as 'invisible friends'. They appear to us in dreams if we give them no more direct channel, and they function as conscience, intuition or hunches, often warning us of imminent danger. They say they are with us from birth and have been with us in other lives. And the feeling of love and familiarity that comes from them is a reality which cannot be denied once felt.

Part of the difficulty in reaching the Inner Guide is that it is so simple. We live in a world which teaches us that for a thing to have value and meaning it should be both difficult to achieve and take a long time to accomplish. The Inner Guide Meditation is both simple and easy, and it can be learned by most people in one experience. The Guide waits for each of us, sometimes throughout an entire lifetime. Our belief that the outer material plane has more value and reality than the inner planes blocks our contact with our personal Guide figures. The Guides are so easy to get to that we've forgotten how. In the distant past the relationship to one's Inner Guide was probably so taken for granted that no one ever thought to write down how to do it.

[1]Carl G. Jung, *Two Essays on Analytical Psychology,* ed. H. Read, M. Fordham, G. Adler, W. McGuire, trans. R. F. C. Hull, *The Collected Works of C. G. Jung,* Bollingen Series XX, vol. 7 (Princeton: Princeton University Press, 1966), p.78-79.

'The Inner Guides come in all the many varieties that we humans do, and they are always *unknown* figures . . . They tend to wear the clothing they wore when they last lived on the planet . . . ' (montage of engravings by Gustave Doré for Coleridge's *The Rime of the Ancient Mariner*).

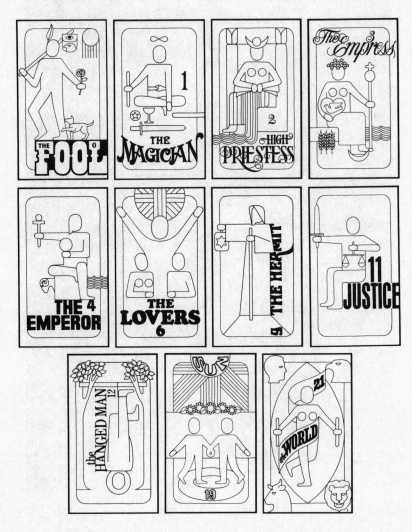

Eleven original Tarot trumps by Karl T. Tani, 1977.

THE
INNER GUIDE MEDITATION
Part II

'The Inner Guides are always human figures and do not have the powers or attributes of gods' (engraving by Gustave Doré from The Bible).

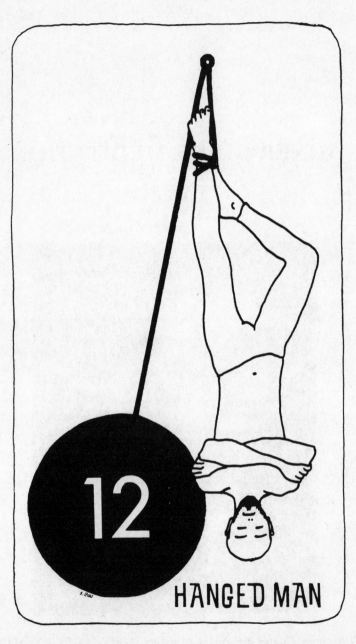

Tarot trump of *The Hanged Man* from the D.O.M.E. Meditation Cards by Sheila W. Ross.

8.

The Inner Guide Contact

Read and follow these instructions carefully

When contacting your Inner Guide for the first time, try not to make it hard or think that you can't do it. A psychological state of ease and relaxation is helpful, though not necessary, for the experience. Sit in a comfortable, straight-backed chair, with your spine erect and both feet flat on the floor. Separate the two sides of the body (don't have your arms or legs touching each other or crossed), with your thighs parallel to the floor and your hands resting lightly on the thighs, palms up and open. Putting the thumb and first finger of each hand together, an Oriental *mudra*, seems to help achieve and maintain a good meditation level for some. Having the left palm up and the right palm down is helpful to others. Experiment to discover which hand positions work best for you.

There seems to be a specific motion sequence or 'movement of the mind' that gets you most easily to the Guide. It is: *forward, then left, and then right.* A movement of forward, left and left tends to bring the false guide. The following visual sequence used for the initial Guide contact is one that has evolved through trial and error over the years. If it doesn't work easily for you, accept a structure that your own unconscious presents to you, or invent your own. There is no way to do it wrong if you follow the above instructions.

Close your eyes, and invent a cave around you as if you have just walked into the cave and the entrance is at your back. Allow the cave to structure itself as it will, well-lighted or dim, smooth-walled or rough. Try to be like blank film receiving impressions. Accept these impressions uncritically as they come to you from this environment. Try not to edit what comes.

Be as *sensory* as you can. Is the cave moist or dry? Feel the weight of your body as you stand on the cave floor. What kind of floor are you standing on? Feel it with your feet. Is it flat and smooth or rough and uneven? Feel the texture of the floor under your feet. Is it sandy, rocky or gravelly? Feel the air around you. Are there currents, or is the air still? Smell the air. Notice the colour impressions that come to you. Use all your senses.

Be sure you are observing and sensing this environment while being *in your body* and *looking out of your eyes.* **Don't be watching an image of yourself!** Should you find yourself watching yourself, get back into your body, **keeping the point of view of your own eyes.** If at any time during the meditation you do find yourself watching your own image, each time return to the viewpoint of your body until it becomes a habit. Feeling the touch of your feet on the ground in the inner world and the weight of your body on your feet will help to keep you in your body, as does the active use of any of your senses.

Keeping the point of view of your own eyes and body is one of the most important aspects of the Inner Guide Meditation. For a long time I couldn't understand why some people weren't getting life results while others were. Then one of the people who got no changes mentioned that he was watching himself and his Guide as if he were watching himself in a film. That was the key. He was 'un-plugged'. If you are only *watching* the meditation process and not actively *in it with all your senses,* the meditation becomes no different than a fantasy or day-dream. You may well get information, but nothing will change, heal or transform in your life. Being *in* your body is essential.

When you can feel yourself in the cave, even though things may still be vague at this point, *move forward and to the left,* away from the cave entrance, and find some kind of doorway or opening there on the left that will lead you out into a landscape. Many people find an actual door in the cave wall. Some go through an arch. Some find a small opening low to the ground that they must crawl through. A few emerge directly into a landscape. Others find a tunnel that leads them out into their landscape. Again, take whatever comes uncritically, and move through the aperture presented by the unconscious.

Take a step out into the landscape when it appears, feeling the new type of ground under your feet. Is it soft or hard, grassy or rocky? What is around you? What is the scene like? Let all these impressions come to you, and let them solidify. What seems to be in the distance? What is the weather like? **Be there as totally as you can.**

Then with your mind call for an animal to come to you. Let it be an animal you don't know (not a familiar house pet or some other known outer world animal e.g., your friend's horse, the neighbour's cat, the lamb you had when you were a child), and ask the animal to lead you off *to the right* to where your Inner Guide awaits you. Concentrate on following the animal, and try not to anticipate the Guide. If the animal appears to meander or stops, give it **permission** to take you *directly* to the feet of your Guide. If you lose sight of the animal or the scene, *will* yourself back to that point where you last saw the animal or scene and allow the action to continue from there. The animals that appear to people come in all varieties. Deer are common, as are squirrels. Sometimes a lion or a dog or cat will appear. People have even had skunks and anteaters. Again, take whatever animal first comes to you, and trust it to be able to lead you to your Inner Guide.

The animal will lead you to the feet of an unknown male figure – your first Guide. The initial Inner Guide for both men and women is an unknown male figure. (This is probably because the horoscopic area which describes his physical being and personality, the Ninth House, is associated with three masculine or *yang* energies: an odd-numbered House, the Ninth; the sign Sagittarius, the natural sign of the Ninth House; and the planet Jupiter, the Ruler of Sagittarius.) You will generally feel an outpouring of love, protection and friendliness from the figure. Many people weep at this point.

Start receiving impressions about the figure. Begin with the feet. Are his feet bare or in some kind of footwear? Then slowly work up the body. Allow impressions of what the figure is like to come to you uncritically, again as if you were blank film. What kind of dress or costume is he wearing? What type of body does he have? Is he fat or thin? Is he tall or short? What kind of hair, if any, does he have? (If the figure is hooded, ask him to throw back the hood.) Is he wearing anything on his head? Is he bearded or clean-shaven? What kind of feeling about him do you get? Is he an active or passive man? Gentle and introverted or extroverted and out-going? Is he dressed in the clothing of any particular occupation or trade or time period? Any particular country or region of the world? Does he hold anything in his hands?

Let all these impressions come to you as they will. Don't *try* to see the Guide's face clearly right away unless it presents itself easily. One of the hallmarks of the true Inner Guide is that his face isn't usually clear at first, although a false guide's face almost always is. The true Guide's face will clear and come into focus later on as you work with him in the meditation process— when you stop trying to 'make him a face'. Be sure to ask the figure if he is your true Guide and if he has the power to protect you in the inner realms. Generally a false guide will answer 'No' to this question or will disappear. Then ask the figure to take both of your hands in his, and give him permission to let you feel his feeling for you. If you don't feel total acceptance and love or caring, you're with a false guide. There is no love from a false guide.

Then ask the Guide to take your right hand in his left. (In left handed people this usually is reversed, the Guide's right hand taking the person's left hand.) *Feel* the hand contact as much as you can. Feel the texture of his skin. Is his hand warm or cool, moist or dry? Is the skin smooth or leathery?

Ask your Guide then to point to where *The Sun* is in the sky of your inner world. Look to where he points. Is *The Sun* right overhead or off to one side? Are there clouds, or does it shine in a clear sky?

At the point where you ask the Guide to point to *The Sun*, a false or ego guide will generally balk, change the subject, try to divert your attention in some way, hedge or will simply vanish. Test for his love again if he remains and your doubts are stirred. If you cannot feel it, stay where you are and look to the right of where the false guide is or was. Another male figure will be there or at least nearby. Feel where the *love* energy comes to you from and creates a warmth in your chest, and look in that direction. Go through the earlier process of allowing him to appear clearly to you, and ignore the false guide if he is still hanging about. If you happen to get a false guide, your true Inner Guide is close by, and if you call for him and give him your permission to come to you, you will probably see him quickly. (The false guides may be either male or female.)

Don't accept any known person from your outer world as your Inner Guide. Your Guide is a being who *wasn't alive on the planet when you were born*, so if your favourite uncle, or your father, or the current or past President of the United States appears, keep looking past him to the right. And if a famous deceased guru or teacher or luminary from the past should appear, test him, and see if another figure appears beyond him on the right.

The Inner Guides come in all the many varieties that we humans do, and they are always **unknown** figures and *not* celebrated spiritual teachers or avatars of the recent or distant past. The Guides tend to wear the clothing they wore when they last lived on the planet (or so they say about themselves), which is perhaps why they seldom appear in contemporary dress. They also say that they are connected to us through love or duty, and that we have shared a life on the planet with them at some time and may well again. And, most important, the **Inner Guides are always human and do not have the powers or attributes of gods**. If a sea serpent, a fairy, an angel or a winged man claims to be your Guide, move past it to the right until your true Guide is encountered.

After your Guide takes your hand and points out where *The Sun* is and you see it, ask *The Sun* to come down, in human form, to where you and your Guide are. Accept the first form it takes. It may come as a male or a female. It might be a man with a bird's head or a swirling mass of colours and energy in humanoid form. It may take the form of Christ, or it may be a dwarf. Try not to preconceive what *The Sun*, as it exists in your inner world, is going to look like. Let it be what it will.

The Sun is the archetype of the **Centre of the Self** – the love-giving, life-giving, creative energy that animates each of us and gives life and motion to the other archetypal forces we carry within us. Our true Inner Guide generally delights in the initial solar contact. Even if *The Sun* energy in your particular horoscopic pattern is weak or repressed, the Guide will do all in his power to bring you into contact with this solar Centre figure so that you can begin the assimilation of this vital energy.

When you and your Inner Guide are together with *The Sun* figure, direct your attention to *The Sun* and ask it to send as much light and love into you physically as you can handle at that particular time. Try to absorb the energy as it comes into

'The animal that leads one to the Inner Guide seems to be related to the *power animals* of shamanism . . .' (engraving by Gustave Doré from La Fontaine's *Fables*).

you. Try not to resist it. It is at this point that most people realize that something *real* and unusual is happening to them that they're *not* 'making up', because they don't know *how* to make up such an experience. This experience of light and love from *The Sun* is often overwhelming, generating tears of joy and is the first inner world experience of a non-ego force. If, by chance, you don't experience this energy physically, give *The Sun* permission to penetrate any blocks that may be up against its energy so that you will be enabled to feel the energy flow within you. Asking the figure to literally *touch* you with its hands or with a directed ray will generally penetrate the blockage and allow you to feel the energy flow.

The two questions that I recommend for use when interacting initially with each of the 22 tarot archetypes are: 1. *What do you need from me and from my life to work with me and be my friend?* and 2. *What do you have to give me* (in the form of a symbolic object placed into your hand) *that I need from you?* The answer to the first question may be a request for a quality such as *Love* or *Trust* or *Honour.* Or it may be a request such as 'Come and visit me daily' or 'Start being kinder to others' or 'Eat more oranges'. Take the first answer that comes into your mind, even if your ego views it as nonsensical. This answer may come in code form to get past the ego's defenses against hearing this information from within. The Inner Guide or the archetype itself may be asked to interpret further or decode its need or request. If you reject the first answer or image that comes to you, ego chatter will follow and confusion will ensue. Try to shut off your normal thinking process and become a receiver. Some of the archetypal forms that, in the psyche, are representative of repressed or suppressed energies may initially appear as 'negative', 'evil' or sickly in the form aspect they present and may request things which are opposed to your moral or ethical values, such as, 'Poison your dog' or 'Shoot the neighbour'. Ask your Guide's advice before agreeing to even seemingly innocent requests, especially if your intuition gives you warning or you 'get a funny feeling' about the request. Refuse those requests your Guide advises you to refuse, and continue asking the archetype's need until you elicit an acceptable request, *one which you feel you can and will fulfill in your everyday life.*

Remember, you're in foreign territory. Trust and use your Inner Guide to act both as interpreter and counsellor – truly let him guide you. Expect from him what you would from a wise teacher. If you become confused or don't understand what's going on there in the inner world, *ask him* to explain. The true Inner Guides don't volunteer any information, so don't hesitate to ask questions in order to get explanations and interpretations. Another thing about the true Guides is that they will judge no one, neither you nor anyone else in your world. Nor will they usually make predictions about you or others. *They will never invade another's privacy in any way.* Should your Guide start agreeing with you that someone in your outer world is a 'bad guy' or 'evil', you're with a false guide. Another thing to look for is the improvement of outer world conditions as you work with your true Guide. These conditions tend to worsen or fall apart when you're working with a false guide. Watch results, and don't be afraid to test the guides and the archetypes. The Inner Guide Meditation is not fragile and can withstand much testing.

The second question that I recommend asking each archetypal form during the first encounter with it is 'What do you have to give me that I need from you?' Ask that the archetype respond by placing a symbolic *object* into your hand. Accept the first object that appears. If it is not clear, ask that the object be brought into focus and made more clear. Again, use your senses. Feel the object. Is it round or square, hollow or solid? What material is it made of? Is it large or small, heavy or light?

When you are clear what the object is, ask the archetypal figure to interpret just what talent, ability or power the object represents. If you regard it as a tool, how do you use it? What effects does it produce in the inner world? In the outer world? *How do you utilize it in your everyday life?*

These initial gifts from the archetypes represent the talents and abilities you were born with having to do specifically with the energy forms that give them to you. You receive the gift in symbol or code form and must then have it decoded. An archetypal gift may have a very common use: 'It will make you more aware of your surroundings' or 'It will keep your neck from getting stiff' or 'It will help you sleep,' or its use may be one associated with the twilight zone of extrasensory perception and magic: 'It will begin to open your third eye' or 'It is the gift of healing with your hands' or 'It will allow you to journey out of the body' or 'It will begin the safe arousal of the Kundalini'. Remember to check with your Inner Guide as to whether or not you should accept what is offered. If he OK's it, be sure that you've asked enough questions so that you understand just what it is you've been given. If you *don't* understand, ask more questions until it is clear to you. Ask both the archetypal giver and your Guide to help you understand the gift and the ways you may use it in both the inner and outer worlds.

When you have really understood the talent or ability, ask the archetype that presented the gift to place it in or on your body at a place where you should absorb and carry it. Feel where the energy form of the object settles within you. This absorption into the body is usually accompanied by unusual physical sensations in one or more parts of the body.

Again, check out all the steps in the process with your Inner Guide. He's there to help you, but *he can't help unless he is asked.* (The Guides will not act spontaneously on their own except when danger to the ego, physical, spiritual or psychological, is encountered.) Nor can he answer unasked questions.

If you utilize the tarot forms of the archetypal energies, you'll finally have at least 22 symbolic gifts or powers in object form scattered throughout your body. (A crystal may be in the centre of your forehead, an apple in the heart, a stick of green wood in the right hand, pearls around the neck, an iron sphere in the genitals, etc.) It is helpful to make an outline of a human body on a sheet of paper and keep it as a record of where each of your symbolic gifts is placed. Experiment with these tools or gifts, and record the results in your journal of meditation experiences, the log of your inner journeys. See if they *do* what you've been told they'll do. If the Tarot *Empress* has given you a copper rod which she explained would do healing, think of a sick plant in your environment, and ask your Inner Guide to bring it to where you and the Tarot *Empress* are in the inner realm. Ask her to show you *how* to heal the plant with the rod, and follow her instructions. Then observe the plant in the outer world. If you see no improvement within two or three days, have your Guide take you back to *The Empress*, explain to her that the plant doesn't seem to be healing, and ask her what you don't understand about using the healing tool or magical implement you were given. **Don't let negative results lie.** Don't rationalize them. Always go to the giver of the ability and challenge the results until your tools work for you. When you've mastered the ability of a certain tool, ask your Guide to take you back to its giver and ask if there is any other power that tool may have that you are unaware of. *These tools or abilities are for use in our everyday lives* – not just on the inner planes.

The two questions that you ask the archetypal energy images at the first encounter and the answers, actions and objects they elicit, serve to indicate to you just *where* that energy is within you (whether positive or negative, conscious or unconscious). It also serves to establish an initial balance between the ego and the energy of the form you touch and work with. At the conclusion of each inner working, remember to ask your Guide if all the energies that you've encountered are in balance or if anything has been left undone. Remember that all *taking from* must be balanced by a *giving to*. To receive from an archetype without giving in return seems to allow that force *carte blanche* to take what it wishes from any area of life as a balancing factor. It's best to know the cost of what you are receiving. The Inner Guide will tell you if all is in balance if you remember to ask him.

I recommend the tarot images as a source of archetypal references because of their correlation to astrology and the individual's natal horoscope. If these images aren't compatible with you, however, use any other symbol keys you like: the pantheon of the Greek gods, the Christian religious archetypes, the Hindu gods, the ancient Egyptian *neters* or 'god' forms, cartoon characters from Disney, figures from fairy tales, the Norse gods. For instance, one friend reported that all the archetypal figures that appeared to her looked like biblical characters, the Tarot *High Priestess* appearing as the Virgin Mary, the Tarot *Sun*, as Jesus.

Whatever figures you choose or that appear initially will start to shift and change as you work with them. They will begin to remold and alter your initial target images, going through your memory banks and utilizing the symbols, forms and images which best express *their* particular energy as it exists in you at the time you are working with and experiencing them. You may begin with an image of the Tarot *Empress* just as she appears in a tarot deck only to find that her form turns into that of a witch stirring a cauldron, and it remains in that altered form no matter how hard you may try to force it back into the tarot original with your mind. Even as the witch figure changes as you interact and work with her from 'evil' seeming to 'good', she will remain uniquely herself, *The Empress* as she lives in *you*, unlike any outer image or symbol.

On occasion the figures will present themselves as pure symbol – the Tarot *Justice* appearing as an ice cube or a pair of scales, *The High Priestess* as a crystal ball, *The Lightning-Struck Tower* as a phallus. Take whatever comes, and try to work with it as it first presents itself. Ask why it is presenting itself in that particular form. What is it trying to communicate to you? It will change as you assimilate its force and its message, sometimes in the middle of a conversation. If you have difficulty working with a talking ice cube, ask the image to take a human form and accept the first one that presents itself. Sometimes this request for a human form is ignored or refused – it was two years before the Tarot *Wheel of Fortune* energy within me would take a human form, although I requested this at each meeting.

The way to assimilate the energies most rapidly into the ego is to get as *involved* in the meditative experience as you can. *Touch the figures.* Utilize all your sensory apparatuses. Voice your disagreements. Complain of their harshness or coldness. Hold onto those who try to leave before the interaction is complete, or call them back or ask your Guide to bring them back if they do depart. For those whose response to your questions is silence, give permission to them to answer your questions whether you want to hear their answers or not. Demand that they answer. When an archetype is silent, it generally indicates that the ego doesn't want to hear the information which that archetype has to give. Insist that an answer be given. Give permission that the answer be given in picture form, and then ask your Guide to help you understand and decode it. The acts of insisting and giving permission enable the ego to push through its own resistances and defence systems. Give the archetypal forms in your inner world the same reality you would grant any 22 individuals in your outer world, and you'll find the changes in your life both rapid and positive.

The side effects of the Inner Guide Meditation are what amaze the ego the most. Psychic ability may suddenly flower without your having worked specifically on the development of that particular talent. Outer world perceptions become acute, and the world literally becomes *new*. The creation energy wells up from within, and a knowledge of a *Oneness* with all becomes a fact of the being. You find yourself automatically thinking: 'Brother George has the flu – I'll have to work inside more' or 'I wonder what part of me caused her to do *that* to me' or 'I'll have to heal that part of myself'. Opposites begin to be perceived as poles of a single unity, and the dance of the archetypal energies becomes a dance in which you are a joyful participant. You find that inner temple within you which has *always* existed to contain and trigger your own personal God experience. And you find yourself *seeing* the beauty and goodness of all the worlds.

The Inner Guide Meditation is a way of working on inner planes that is a direct outgrowth of what is referred to as the Western Mystery Tradition. It is an action oriented method: you move, you utilize your ego and your senses, you ask questions and challenge, you barter and exchange, you argue, you insist, you explore, you discover, you laugh and you cry. It is the method of the Child in us all – open and direct. And it can be used by anyone, anywhere. Children, from about seven years of age on, love the Inner Guide Meditation and take to it like fish to water. The elderly can use it as easily as the young. The rules are those that you and your Guide establish. They change only as that **YOU** that goes on from life to life and never dies, gently takes over the reins of your life, and the ego and Self work in unity. There is no need for the outer teacher; you carry your own instructor and spiritual mentor within. *Allow him to teach you.* There is no need to project the Guide onto any outer figure; doctor, priest, astrologer, scientist, minister or politician, once you have contacted him in your own inner world. The Kingdom of Heaven is *truly* within you, and your Inner Guide will show you *your* way.

Something I should mention at this point is that there seem to be four primary Guides within, corresponding to different vibrational levels of the inner reality. The first Guide is the male figure I have already mentioned. The next two Guides are usually, but not always, men. The fourth Guide is usually a woman. I mention this here so that there will be no confusion when your first Inner Guide, who will probably work with you for quite a long time (I was with my first Guide, Aman, for four years), indicates that you will be going on to a new Guide. Different people are directed to the second Inner Guide at different times and in different ways. The first Guide generally initiates the meeting. Sometimes it is spontaneous or occurs in a dream. It may take many years to reach a new Guide for some – few for others. One factor seems to be how quickly the

physical system, a part of the ego, is safely able to assimilate the
archetypal energies and respond with a change in the mind-
body vehicle. Another factor is the ego's acceptance of the fact
that the energies it contains are generating the entire reality it
is experiencing, and that it alone is *responsible for*, although *not to
blame for,* all that is occurring in the outer reality. The
individual's psychic aspect (tenanted Water Signs and Houses
in the horoscope) and the amount of ego resistance and
scepticism to be pushed through are also factors.

If a new Guide appears suddenly without any previous
indication of his coming, test the authenticity of the figure with
your current Guide. Often when the ego finds itself changing
as a result of the inner work, it will unconsciously call forth a
false guide to attempt to slow down or to stop the transformation process. These false or ego guides are the flatterers
and the liars and go along with the ego's rationalization
process. They will tell the ego whatever it needs to hear to
sabotage the spiritual evolutionary process. Whenever you are
in a transition from one Guide to the next, check out the new
Guide with the Guide you have been working with. This
testing process has been found to avoid major detours in the
inner working.

There are many ways to work with your Inner Guide. You
can just turn yourself over to him as your inner guru or
spiritual teacher and ask him to teach you in whatever way is
best for you. If you have had a dream or a nightmare that you
would like to understand and work with, ask the Guide to set
up a screening booth and ask him to re-run the dream for you,
treating it like a movie you're watching. Stop the action as you
wish, and ask your Guide to interpret the various episodes for
you. The Inner Guides are skilled and wise dream interpreters.
When you finish with the interpretation of the dream or
nightmare, ask your Guide whether or not you and he should
go back *into* the dream and change, fix, complete or heal any
portion of it. Follow the same process of working with dream
figures as you do with the archetypes. Dream figures that
appear as evil, diseased, dying or dead, often symbolize those
aspects of ourselves which need the most love and attention
from our egos. They represent energies repressed or suppressed within us. Should the Guide recommend a healing or
a transformation of one of these inner dream figures, ask him
to call forth the Tarot *Sun* archetype, and ask *The Sun* to send its

light-love energy into the image that requires the healing or transformation until it changes or resurrects. Remember that *everything and everyone in your dreams represents some aspect of yourself.* If you dream of a known person from your outer world, that person is one of your projection screens, living out in the outer and the inner worlds some aspect of yourself.

Never work in the inner world with known figures from your outer reality! If a known figure appears in a meditation or in a dream (your mother, your brother, the woman-next-door), before you work with the energy the known figure represents, *ask that the image of this person takes its true form as it lives in you,* not as he or she appears or has appeared in your outer world reality. Working with a known figure from your outer world in the inner world or trying to force a person from your outer world to do something you wish him to do in the meditation process without that person's *knowledge and ego permission in the outer world* amounts to black magic. This will draw commensurate dues for you to pay, usually in the form of headaches or nausea, but often much more extreme. 'Messing with someone's mind' or with his actions or will without the person's ego consent is against Universal Law, and the Law is enforced. Even if you're tempted to do what you consider to be 'good' for another, such as healing an illness or helping in your inner world to get the person a job in the outer world, *ask permission first* of the person involved *in the outer world.* And ask your Guide's advice also on such projects. The best way to help someone who is troubled or in pain in your outer world is to ask the image of the individual to take its true form as it lives within you, and then heal or transform that part of yourself which unconsciously participates in the outer individual's 'bad trip'. But remember, once the image is in its true form, it is a picture of the energy that went out of you and manipulated that person as a character in your movie – it no longer has anything to do with the outer world person. It is now a picture of an energy aspect of yourself, and try to remember that *this* is what you are healing or transforming – a real part of yourself unconnected to anyone else.

Another way to work with the Inner Guides is in terms of the events in your everyday life. If you find yourself in some hassle or painful life situation, ask your Guide to take you to the inner energy image that is causing the outer problem. If you are working with the tarot figures or with your horoscope, resist the temptation to figure out or preconceive what single figure or group of figures may be the culprits. Remember that the tarot images are pictures of energies. These energies can combine and re-combine, and perhaps the figure the Guide takes you to will be one you have never encountered before. It may be composed of two parts Tarot *High Priestess* energy, one part Tarot *World* and three parts Tarot *Chariot.* Accept whatever form the Guide brings or leads you to, and work with that form. Trust your Inner Guide to take you to the composite image of all the forces associated with the particular life situation you are dealing with, and work with whatever he presents. *Try not to guide your Guide* or he becomes ineffectual in his role.

If you want a systematic way to work and don't have a tarot-horoscope equivalent worksheet, you can begin with the tarot images by starting with *The Fool* image and working forward through the Major Arcana with each of the archetypal energies in turn, or you can work backwards from the Tarot *World* figure, last of the Trumps. (See the list of archetypes at the back of the book.) The figures will not generally appear as they do in the tarot card images, and even if they do at first, they will soon begin to change as you interact with them.

Never go into the inner world without your Inner Guide. It can be dangerous for you and could possibly blow all the circuits much like a bad acid trip. There is no such thing as losing your Guide once you've contacted him. If your Guide seems to have disappeared while you are working with him, just call for him and he'll be there. *Don't look for him.* The act of looking is full of ego imposition and is generally unsuccessful in locating the Guide's presence. *Allow* him to be there. He'll be there with you, and *feel* his presence.

Sometimes our ego's resistances will put harmless blocks in our way to the Inner Guide in the form of brick walls, monsters standing in our path, people we know attempting to distract us and lead us in another direction. **Ignore them.** Give them no energy. Walk *through* the walls or monsters. Disregard those who appear before you have come to your Guide. There is no danger in the unconscious until we are *beyond* the place where we meet our Guide, and beyond the meeting place (which you should establish with your Guide during the initial meditation) the Inner Guide is with us as our protector from potential dangers.

Another resistance trick you may experience comes from without. Just as you are about to sit down to meditate, your environment may go crazy: the dog will bark, the telephone will ring, an unexpected visitor will knock on the door, someone will break something in the next room, the cat will get into a fight outside your window, etc. This resistance pattern lasts for about two weeks, if you encounter it at all, and, if you find it happening, try to prepare for it in advance as much as you can to insure a quiet meditation period.

Remember also that the Inner Guides are always human figures. They are not gods and have no god-like powers of their own (although they may have the ability to fly, float or walk through walls.) They neither judge nor flatter. They may have personality traits which seem at first most un-Guide-like. My first guide, Aman, always seemed rather spaced out and absent-minded. The qualities they seem to share are their protection of us, their love and concern for us and our spiritual growth, and their guidance towards the realization of our own Centre or God-aspect. Everyone loves his or her Inner Guide in a very personal, ego-involved way. In fact you can develop such a strong love and attachment to your initial Guide that when it is time to go on to the next Guide, you may have to overcome your own ego's resistance to the transition – much like having to separate from some much loved friend in your outer world.

Drugs of any kind (alcohol, marijuana, heroin, opium, cocaine, hashish, barbituates, THC, amphetamines and the like) will interfere with or block the Guide contact and sabotage the meditation. Try to not have any alcohol on the day you are to first contact your Guide, if you are being initiated by a D.O.M.E. Inner Guide Initiator, or for at least two weeks if you are working alone. Marijuana tends to stay in the body as a blockage for from eight to fourteen days or longer and weakens or prevents the contact with the true Guide. The other drugs in use in our culture vary in their blockage abilities. For a clear initial contact with your Inner Guide try to have your body and nervous system as pure as possible. The natural organic drugs have a tendency to stay in the body and cause blockage effects for a longer period of time than the chemical drugs, so allow sufficient time for your body to expel them if you are into drugs.

Insist on the availability of all your senses when working with the

Inner Guide Meditation, and *always use them* – especially seeing and hearing. There are many speakers within. Be sure you are *seeing* the speaker. Keep the meditation experience fully sensory. For example, the Tarot *High Priestess* may be giving you important information and may sound as though she is in good shape within you, but without your vision you would not see that she is weeping as she speaks.

Many people ask if they should study and read about the tarot figures before they attempt the Inner Guide Meditation and the working with the inner images and energies that the tarot represents. I would generally advise people *not* to read or study the tarot until they have *experienced* each of the tarot energy forms at least once. It becomes impressive to a sceptical ego to read about what they *should* be like *after* the initial experiences with them. The tarot archetypes are *living* energies. As our horoscopes demonstrate by accurately describing our individual realities, these archetypes are creating and sustaining us, not vice versa. We seem to have learned everything exactly backwards about the way reality-generating energies actually flow. The archetypes always *are* as they *should be*. There is no other choice for them. They are first, we are second and the rest of reality is third.

It is also impressive after the experiences with the archetypes to have an astrologer explain directly from your own natal horoscopic pattern *why* the Tarot *Last Judgement* figure appeared to you as a jackal, why it gave you a butterfly, and why the figure placed the symbol into your genitals. It is just as if you had studied all the tarot-astrology symbolism beforehand, expressing it directly according to astrological theory and symbolism.

We live in a culture that teaches us that we should know about things in advance, but this seems to interfere with, more than aid, the Inner Guide Meditation. We are already pro-grammed with enough 'shoulds'. Going inside with ego information about how the archetypes 'should be', 'should look' and 'should act' will often interfere with how they *are*, how they *do* look, how they *do* act, as they present themselves in the individual psyche. If you can take it on faith in the beginning, even if you think 'I'm making this all up' or 'This is silly', and can really trust your Guide, you will be more impressed later on with the information you receive. Working without preconceptions is somewhat difficult, especially for us in Western civilization, but it is the most rewarding way in the long run.

If an inner tester whispers, 'You're making this all up,' respond with, 'Making it all up from *where?*' The images, the feelings, the thoughts that come can only arise from your own psycho-spiritual system. Continue 'making it up', if you think that's what you're doing, and you'll find the results and changes in your outer world astonishing – as if circles of healing light were touching and changing everyone and everything around you, effecting your whole environment.

Remember – it's the movie that *your* energies are creating that you think of as reality.

The Inner Guide Meditation doesn't seem to interfere with any other way of meditating or 'working inside'. Nor does it seem to be incompatible with any religious system except for the most dogmatic and insecure. If you are a Christian, it deepens your understanding of Christ. If you are into Yoga, the Guide smooths your way. The Jew becomes a better Jew. The Humanist, more humane. And the atheist or agnostic experiences the spiritual, perhaps for the first time.

The Inner Guide Meditation places spiritual authority back *within* the individual – its true and holy place. Your Guide exists to teach you *your* spiritual path, *your* way to God, not someone else's.

9.

False Guides

False or ego guides are enough of a problem for people with a lot of resistance to their own transformation process, that I wish to reiterate and add to the information already given about them.

First of all, let no one claiming psychic powers or claiming knowledge superior to your own tell you that your Guide is false, unless they are a trained Inner Guide Meditation Initiator with a certificate of competence from D.O.M.E., the Inner Guide Meditation Center in Colorado. If you do not have access to such a trained Initiator, trust yourself. The information contained in this book is complete. Be thorough in your reading and your understanding of the material given herein. Take time to digest it all before beginning the initial Guide contact; especially study the 'Questions and Answers' section that follows.

Second, the test of love is the test of the true Guide. If consistently there is no feeling of love and total acceptance from a figure you have contacted and think to be your Guide, you are probably working with a false guide. Go back to where you first met him, and feel beyond him to your right for the love from your true Guide. He will come when you let him.

False guides are often judgmental of you or others, or they will inflate your ego using flattery. They will encourage separative thinking, most often telling you that you are 'right' and others are 'wrong'. They give no new insights, and they subtly discourage ego change and growth, attempting to help the ego maintain its *status quo*. Interestingly enough, false guides seem to be reflections of the current ego, with all its defenses and hang-ups. Your true Guide will probably, though not always, have a personality much different than your own. His point of view will also be very different than yours. If you and a figure you think may be your Guide think exactly alike, he is probably a false guide.

Another way to see whether or not you have a false guide is to ask yourself if your life has changed since you began working with him. If there have been no changes, you are probably with a false guide.

If you have continued doubts about the figure you have contacted, who has presented himself to you as your true Guide, you might also write to us at D.O.M.E. with a description of the figure you have contacted along with a description of other figures you might have encountered when you first attempted to contact your Guide. Send this inform-ation along with an application for your horoscope and Astrology-Tarot Equivalent Worksheet (information at back of book), and the D.O.M.E. staff will check to see if the figure you are working with coincides with the description of the Inner Guide from your natal horoscope. Remember to include as many details about the figure as you can, e.g., appearance, personality, age, personal qualities, clothing, body type, hair, eye colour and qualities, ornaments worn, etc. If the figure wears a hooded robe, ask him to throw back the hood so that you can get impressions of his head and perhaps see some details about his face, even though you might not see the whole face clearly.

STOP!

BEFORE READING FURTHER IN THIS BOOK, STOP AND THINK. HAVE YOU UNDERSTOOD ALL THE INFORMATION AND CONCEPTS UP TO THIS POINT? IF ANYTHING UP TO NOW HAS BEEN VAGUE OR FUZZY, GO BACK AND REREAD PARTS I AND II BEFORE CONTINUING.

Remember that it is most important that your psycho-physical system be as purified as possible before attempting Inner

Guide Meditation. Stay off all drugs which might inhibit initial
Inner Guide contact, especially marijuana, and use no alcohol
for at least two weeks before attempting the initial contact.
Think of yourself as a temple being prepared and cleansed to
welcome the arrival of a true and holy spiritual teacher.

It is also advised that before contacting your Guide initially
that you read and absorb the remainder of this book. There is
much that is contained in the 'Questions and Answers' section
that will help you with the initial contact and further your
working with your Inner Guide. The 'Questions and Answers'
also contain important information that will let you get the
'feel' of the meditation through questions and reactions others
have had.

I would also advise rereading the book at least monthly for
the first three to six months of regular meditation. As you work
with the meditation and evolve your own meditation rhythm,
the rereading will cause you to be aware of material you may
have not assimilated or didn't think you needed to remember
during the early stages of your meditation practice.

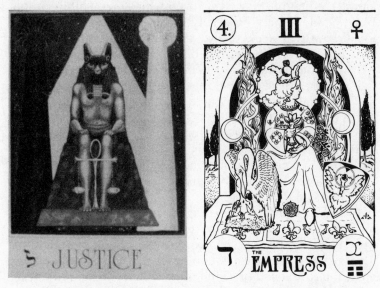

Tarot Trump *Justice* from the Servants of the Light Tarot Deck.

Trump of *The Empress* from the Jerry Kay *Book of Thoth* Tarot Deck.

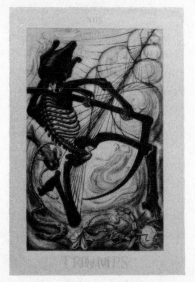

Trump of *Death* from the Crowley Tarot Deck.

Trump of *The Chariot* from the Crowley Tarot Deck.

THE
INNER GUIDE MEDITATION
Part III

'Zeus disguised himself in the form of an eagle and abducted Ganymede, carrying him off to Mount Olympus' (engraving by Gustave Doré from Dante's *Purgatory*).

'Marriage is the unconscious agreement on the part of two individuals to accept each other's Shadow projection and live it out (engraving by Gustave Doré from Milton's *Paradise Lost*).

10.

Questions and Answers

1.   Q. Is the Inner Guide Meditation just common sense?

A. 'Common sense' has little to do with it. Because we are still ignorant of the physics involved in the relationships between the inner and outer realities, the archetypes frequently make requests or suggest actions that may seem irrational. For instance, an archetype might tell one that to plant flowers or to re-position one's bed will solve a certain health problem, and it does. These energies exhibit a multi-dimensional symbol physics we don't yet understand.

2.   Q. What is the best attitude to approach the Inner Guide Meditation with?

A. Let each meditation be new, fresh, unexpected. Try not to compare your meditations to each other or to anyone else's meditations. Try not to anticipate what will happen. Let it flow by itself under your Guide's direction. **Don't guide your Guide.**

3.   Q. Is the Inner Guide always a positive figure?

A. I've talked to some people who have initially had a disapproving ego reaction to some aspect of the Guide, but even these people end up loving their Guide. Everyone loves the true Guide. It's the essential part of the relationship. The most crucial factor determining whether we have a positive or negative reaction to the Guide initially seems to be the degree to which we project the Guide outside of ourselves onto others.

4.   Q. Why do you emphasise the Tarot *Sun* and *Fool* as being
       so important in terms of the inner work?

       A. Although all the tarot forces or archetypes are ways of
       perceiving aspects of the God energy, the Tarot *Fool* and
       Sun represent the Centre pole. Both are aspects of love
       energy. The *Sun* is our life-giving essence – the Centre of
       the Self, the Prime Mover within. The Tarot *Fool* re-
       presents freedom, friendship and altruistic love – the
       love of all humanity without discrimination. The more
       you work with these particular energies, the more you
       will find that your base transfers itself from ego to Centre.
       That's why I consider it important to concentrate on the
       Tarot *Sun* and *Fool* in inner work. Their combined love
       energies will heal and transform the most negative
       appearing archetypal energy forms.

5.   Q. Is the Inner Guide Meditation essentially a spiritual
       discipline or does it have materialistic uses?

       A. The Inner Guide Meditation is a spiritual discipline,
       but I've worked with people whose primary current
       ego interest was making money or finding a partner.
       The Guides accept us on whatever level we operate,
       whatever our current values may be, and they help
       us work toward an understanding of our life and
       goals. What I usually find is that the Guides subtly direct
       us toward our own inner spiritual goals as we continue to
       work with them whether we are initially conscious of this
       or not.

6.   Q. Does the Inner Guide Meditation have any influence
       over physical disease?

       A. It seems to work dramatically with physical diseases,
       but much research will have to be done in this area.
       People have reported all sorts of 'miraculous' healings,
       such as the absorption of tumours, the remission of
       cancer, bones mending overnight, ulcers disappearing
       and the like.
          I had an experience with an abscessed tooth that had
       swollen my right jaw and was painfully throbbing. When
       I worked on it in meditation, the Guide first had me

Trump of *The High Priestess* from the Crowley Tarot Deck.

Trump of *The Magician* from the Rider-Waite Tarot Deck.

Trump of *The Emperor* from the Crowley Tarot Deck.

The Wheel of Fortune and *The Sun* as a child as they might appear and relate in an Inner Guide Meditation (engraving by Gustave Doré from La Fontaine's *Fables*).

literally separate the pain from my physical body by moving it two feet away from myself. When I was able to do this, the Tarot *Sun* form came and healed it. The problem had gone within half an hour. X-rays I had months afterwards showed no evidence that there had ever been an abscess in that area or any cause for one.

Usually healings happen as side effects of the meditation, rather than anything as dramatic as the previous mentioned experience. However, physical problems that we are taught to think of as permanent or incurable often disappear, remit or heal as we work with our Guides and the archetypes.

7.   Q. Are there any other physical results from working with this meditation?

A. As you work with the energies through the Inner Guide Meditation, you will find yourself changing physically. You will start craving foods that you disliked before or lose your taste for foods that you liked. The dietary change is one of the first things you'll notice when you're working with the archetypes and the Guide. I had been meditating for about six months when red meat 'went away'. This wasn't the result of any philosophical decision or insight. I would order a steak or a hamburger out of habit, then find that I couldn't eat it. Chicken and fish soon followed as I sort of involuntarily became a vegetarian.

8.   Q. Why does dietary change occur as a result of the Inner Guide Meditation?

A. I suspect that the sensations, often unusual, experienced in the physical body as the archetypal energies touch us and we interact with them result from real changes in our cells and their needs. The cells develop new nourishment needs, needs for new minerals and nutrients, new balances. *Spiritual change is physical change.* To project a new reality or to change the current hologram, the projection unit itself, the physical vehicle, must be changed. As the cells call out for new foods, we respond by seeking them out and losing interest in the old.

9.   Q. I'm able to see the Guide and the archetypes outside of me, projected around me into my environment. Is it all right to work with them in this way?

A. This is much like laying out the tarot cards and reading them. When the forces are projected outside of us, our egos are able to filter and control them too easily. *The Secret of the Golden Flower* tells why it is necessary to focus inwardly. This secret is that we must learn to make the *light* flow backward, to follow the energy that projects *out* of us *back toward its source* – to face *toward* the sources of the archetypal energies. In this manner the ego is able to filter and control less, and we receive truer information and more unexpected insights. *Always work inside.*

10.   Q. Why do you say it is important to record Inner Guide Meditations and dreams?

A. Writing down meditations and dreams helps to bring the inner energies out into daily life – to *earth* them. It also prevents the trickster, the human mind under the ego's control, from juggling, forgetting or editing our inner experiences (both dreams and meditations). Recording this inner material furthers the interchange between the inner and outer worlds. This interchange can be likened to an infinity sign, one loop being the inner world, the other, the outer. A written record serves as good eye evidence of this interplay.

11.   Q. Sometimes I get fruit or vegetables from the archetypes. What does this mean?

A. This often indicates a dietary need. Ask the Guide and the archetype that gives the fruit or vegetable if this is what is being indicated. For instance, people with strong Uranian or Aquarian elements in their patterns are often given apples. Apples seem to calm the electrical system. under the rulership of Aquarius *(The Star)* and Uranus *(The Fool)*. Experiments with this inner world information seem to indicate that apple juice doesn't work unless freshly prepared, and that apples should be eaten between meals and not mixed with other foods.

V

The Hierophant

Trump of *The Hierophant* from the Crowley Tarot Deck.

12.   Q. My mind keeps drifting or sometimes I fall asleep while meditating. What can I do about this?

A. This is usually caused by the archetypal forces called *The Hanged Man* and *The Moon* in tarot (Neptune and Pisces in astrology). If you ask the Guide to take you to the images of these two energies within and talk to them about the problems of concentration and alertness, you should be able to obtain a solution to the problem. The phenomena you mention seem to indicate a repression of one or both of these energies or a repression of energies connected to the Twelfth House. They have to do with our escapist urges; spacing out, fantasizing, day-dreaming.

The archetypes often suggest a more *active* fantasy life, with you *entering* the fantasy with the Guide and *participating* rather than merely watching yourself on an inner movie screen or stage. Fantasizing and day-dreaming, where you are only the observer, are among the greatest thieves of life energy. The remedy for this seems to be *getting into it and living it* on the inner planes with your Guide. Then you provide a doorway for the energy to come into your daily life on the earth plane.

13.   Q. Can two people work together with the Inner Guide Meditation?

A. Yes, definitely. This works well with someone who knows what you want to work with, the questions you want to ask, and the kinds of things you want to accomplish. Have the other person record for you when you meditate, and you record for him when he meditates.

People working in tandem this way seem to experience an accelerated growth. When someone is writing down the experience for you, you can get into the experience more fully without having to consciously attempt to remember all the details. The experience of the inner planes is much like the experience of a dream. When you come back, details tend to fall back into unconsciousness just as they do with dreams. Another problem this solves is that of getting so involved with one experience that you forget the other things you wanted to do in meditation.

If you are working with someone personally involved

with you, your husband or wife, for instance, be aware that there will be tendency to try to maintain each other's projected role relationships. The person recording might try to guide the Guide in accordance with the wishes of his own ego, conscious or unconscious. This will be less of a problem if both persons are aware of this tendency and verbalize it. Though the Guides will usually take care of such outside interference, always trust your Inner Guide over any outer figure acting as a guide or counsellor.

14. Q. I'm working with a psychologist who is against my utilizing the Inner Guide Meditation. How should I deal with this?

A. The Inner Guide Meditation can be threatening not only to psychiatrists and psychological counsellors in general, but also to astrologers and leaders of spiritual groups. If you work with your Guide regularly, there is usually little need to continue with an outer guide for long, unless you need the additional ego support, wish to accelerate the inner process, or wish to develop more rapidly some latent talent or ability. If you have an accurately calculated horoscope and can translate it yourself or get it translated into tarot terms, you have the road map of your essential structure, inner and outer. The Guide can do the rest. He is your teacher. The Inner Guide Meditation, or any other do-it-yourself meditation method for that matter, can also represent an economic threat to many of us in the counselling professions.

As with any new idea, the Inner Guide Meditation meets with resistance in established quarters. Some psychologists equate the Inner Guide Meditation with Jungian 'active imagination', a potentially dangerous method. The Guides, however, prevent these dangers by their protective presence and knowledgeable guidance.

Ask your Guide why your psychiatrist objects and what energy within *you* is causing his objection.

15. Q. Does the Inner Guide Meditation lower one's resistance to 'the powers of darkness' or 'the lower astral'?

A. No. The contrary seems to be true. Working with the

Guide, and especially those tarot archetypes associated with light, such as *The Sun, The Fool, The Star* and *Tarot Strength*, in a truth-seeking manner, seems to attract fewer and fewer negative elements into one's life. I've never known a Guide to advise or encourage anyone on a power trip, especially of the 'black magic' variety.

The Guides will not interfere with us, nor will they aid or direct us toward dark paths or ways of unconsciousness. They *will* let us set up unconscious situations if we don't ask their advice, and they will not interfere in these situations unasked unless there is a possibility of physical death or irreparable harm to the ego. Good teachers will often let their charges fall flat on their faces when they're not asked for assistance or instruction.

16. Q. Why don't I get life results that others claim to get? The results I get sometimes seem negative to me.

A. Perhaps this is due to ego resistance or to working with a false or ego guide. If you aren't getting results in the form of positive life changes from the Inner Guide Meditation (and usually they are quite rapid, positive and dramatic), and if you've been working regularly, ask the Guide to take you to that part of you that is preventing the life changes from happening or to those parts of you that are not being heard or accepted.

Also, the ego is not always the best judge of results in the long run. Sometimes people tell me: 'I began working with my Guide, and my whole world fell apart'. Though this may be quite true, in a few cases, the world that fell apart generally turns out to have been a frozen reality that prevented the individual's growth and evolution, while the world coming in and replacing the old is an open-ended one with an infinity of possibilities, material and spiritual. Often what the ego holds onto most desperately is exactly what is preventing its own growth and change.

Challenge the Guide for explanations of outer life changes, especially if they seem negative to you. If you ask why, he'll explain.

Outer physical reality corresponds *exactly* to the inner energy structures – to the inner reality. If negative results occur in your outer life, demand to confront their sources within.

17.   Q. I find myself sceptical of the Inner Guide Meditation itself and the results other people tell me about. How can I overcome this?

A. Scepticism, fear, doubt and judgement are generally caused by the forces which are called in the tarot *The World* and *Old Pan* or *The Devil* (the Saturn and Capricorn energies in astrology). If you meet and interact with these energy forms on the inner planes, you should find that your scepticism abates.

The Saturn and Capricorn energies we all carry are part of our safety systems. They are the energies that *test* our egos and our realities. Their job is to maintain our limits and our structures, on all levels, until we are experienced enough and strong enough to change or go beyond them. They want to make sure we miss no steps. We often think of them as the 'bad guys' within, but, in fact, they function in their ways as protectors. These two energies project out of us onto Father, boss, the police-man, the Establishment, career, reputation and the Law. They represent the living bone of our reality structures. The only proof that Saturn and Capricorn accept is that of living experience in our everyday lives.

So if you're sceptical of others' results, try the medi-tation yourself over a period of time and see what happens. 'The fruit of the tree' is the only real proof of any spiritual system.

18.   Q. How can I be sure that the Guide and the contact with him and the archetypes are real?

A. In lieu of the horoscope, which describes the appear-ance and personality of the Guide, accept the Guide figure that presents himself and go by your feelings. If you really feel love and protection coming from him, work with him. Have him take you to the archetypes within. See what happens in your outer world as you work with him. The test of the real Guide is what happens in your daily life, what happens around you.

After reading many horoscopes and initiating many

people into the Inner Guide Meditation, I'm beginning
to see that we *can't* make anything up, even though the
ego may tell us we can. In initiation after initiation,
people often think they are 'making up the whole thing',
but, in fact, what they see, hear and feel inside corresponds exactly to their personal horoscopic symbolism,
usually without prior knowledge of astrology or the tarot
as it applies to them.

A technique I recommend to firm up the Guide
contact is to ask the Guide to take *both* of your hands into
his, and then to give him permission to let you *feel* his
feelings for you. With the true Guide you will *always* sense
his love and protectiveness and care. You will not sense
this with a false guide.

19.   Q. 'Forward, left, then right' seems too pat a formula.
How do you explain it?

A. I arrived at this 'movement of the mind' through
experimentation with many different directional
approaches. Through this trial and error method, I
found that this is the one sequence that always works,
pragmatically, in contacting the initial true Guide. I don't
know why it works.

20.   Q. My main difficulty is inertia – making myself do the
meditation. How can I overcome this?

A. I discovered this tendency in myself during one period
of Inner Guide work. I corrected it with the device of
setting daily appointments with myself at specific times
to do the inner work. This structuring of time *utilizes* the
same force that *causes* resistance, Saturn, the Tarot *World.*
Saturn cannot stand to waste time. If you allot a certain
daily time span, you'll find that you won't just sit and do
nothing – you'll meditate. Another way is to work with
someone else, again, on a definite schedule where you
record for them and they record for you. The commit-
ment to others seems to help many, who otherwise
procrastinate.

21.   Q. What is the relation between my archetypes and those
of other people?

A. The archetypes are universal energies. Although we speak about 'my *High Priestess*' and 'your *High Priestess*', there is only one energy in the universe that the Tarot *High Priestess* stands for as a symbol. That energy exists in and flows through all creation, as do the energies of all the other archetypes. If we picture the unconscious as an ocean containing all the archetypal forces and each of us as wave peaks of that ocean receiving the archetypal images in our individual ways, we can begin to get a clearer understanding of how we perceive these energies. There is only one energy corresponding to each of the tarot symbol forms. Our personal patterns, illustrated by our individual horoscopes, determine how each archetype manifests itself to our personal ego views, e.g., the form that a *High Priestess* of a Moon in Gemini will be different than the form of a *High Priestess* of a Moon in Aquarius although the *High Priestess* archetypal energy in both is the same. You might think of it as one colour light coming through two different coloured filters.

22. Q. When an archetype places a symbolic gift into the body, does it make a difference whether it is placed on the right or left side?

A. The gifts that are placed into the left side of the body seem to be abilities, aptitudes or powers that function automatically, like our breathing or heart action. Those that are placed into the right side of the body seem to require an act of will to make them function. Those that are centrally located seem to partake of both the unconscious and ego-conscious qualities (This may be reversed in left-handed people, but I haven't studied a sufficient amount of data on left-handed people to determine whether this is true or not. Information on this point would be greatly appreciated.)

23. Q. Define the ego more specifically.

A. The ego is a process – *current ego* would be a more accurate term. It is like a body-mind membrane that energies flow through and affect. I understand it best in terms of the Cusp of the First House or Point of the Ascendant (often called the Rising Sign) in the individual horoscope. It is our physical vehicle and includes our *persona*, the mask worn in life through which we relate to others. It is who we see when we look in a mirror, our idea of who we are and what we look like. It has a certain material continuity but adapts and changes according to which forces are flowing through and affecting it. The ego at noon is not the same as the ego at midnight. At different times it experiences thoughts, feelings, emotion and objective reality differently. It is a reactive part of the Self. Its material manifestation allows it to perceive and experience the flow of reality in an orderly manner. It contains our point of view and acts as a filter through which we perceive external and internal realities, the kind of coloured glasses through which we look.

24.   Q. When and how often should I do the Inner Guide Meditation?

A. Meditation requires concentration. If there is a tendency to become sleepy or to lack the necessary concentration early in the morning or late at night, I would advise meditating during that part of the day when you are most alert. Your Guide can advise you on this.

Regular meditation, as often as prescribed by the Guide, is important. Getting into a meditation *rhythm* helps to develop inner concentration and the ability to focus easily.

25.   Q. Can I continue working with the animal that first took me to the Inner Guide?

A. The animals that lead us to the Guides were a suggestion from a psychiatrist in Santa Fe, New Mexico, who presented the paper, *The Inner Guide to the Archetypes*, to the Annual Conference of the Society of Jungian Analysts of Northern and Southern California in March, 1972. He and I had both been having difficulty in getting people to move from the point where one leaves the cave and enters the landscape to the point where one meets the Guide. He came up with the idea of calling an animal (a symbol for the instincts or the feeling nature) to lead the way.

The animal that leads one to the Inner Guide seems to

be related to the *power animals* of shamanism and can be used as such with the OK of the Guide. (Michael Harner's *The Way of the Shaman*, Harper & Row, New York, 1980, discusses this at length.)

Since the introduction of the animal into the meditation technique, there has been little difficulty in getting people to their Guides. If you should lose contact while the animal is taking you to the Guide, remember to go back and re-create the scene *where you last saw the animal*. Let it continue from there, even if you have to do this repeatedly. If you wander aimlessly, give the animal *permission* to take you *directly* to the Guide, permission to penetrate any unconscious blockage that may be being created, and then try to see *where* in the landscape the animal seems to be leading you.

If asked, your Inner Guide can tell you whether or not you should continue to use the animal and can also give you additional advice concerning the most efficient method of contacting him. Setting up a specific *meeting place* in the inner landscape to meet the Guide each time you meditate seems to be helpful in reestablishing contact for future meditations.

26.   Q. My main difficulty is in seeing the figures. What can I do about this?

A. I find that if you are with the Guide and a figure that is very nebulous presents itself, it will usually cooperate if you ask it to appear more clearly or give it permission to do so. This will generally be a figure that represents a repressed or suppressed energy. If this phenomenon occurs with all the figures, just pesevere in the meditation, and they will become clearer. Through practice, you will get used to operating in the inner world and will develop the senses that operate there.

There seem to be two ways of *seeing* on the inner planes. Some people have a highly developed visual sense and see as clearly within as they do in a dream or in outer reality. Others, more commonly, don't have this acute visual ability at first, but they are still capable of describing minute details of the scene or figure they are experiencing. They describe their way of seeing as 'imagining', 'knowing', 'getting a mental picture' or 'seeing with the mind's eye'. Accept whatever you see in the meditation, however you see it. Don't compare your meditations or visual experiences with others. You are unique. See as *you* see. Often, as you meditate for a length of time, clear and colourful visual images will appear and fade. Let them come and go as they will. Take what you get. Remember to *receive* the images as if you were blank film receiving impressions. **Don't look – receive;** and learn to accept the *first* image that comes.

27. Q. How can I get a clear answer from my Inner Guide and the archetypes?

A. Give them permission to tell you the answer to your question *whether you want to hear the answer or not.* Frequently, our own resistance to the information that the Guide, the 'Shadow' or an archetype holds for us causes the lack of an answer. Insisting that you want to know and pushing through your own ego resistance for the answer will almost always bring it forth.

You can also ask them to write the answer or make words appear in the air before you – or ask for a picture or a symbol that represents the answer, then let your Guide decipher it for you. On some greatly resisted material in myself and others I have asked that a home movie screen be set up in the inner world and images (that can then be decoded by the Guide if necessary) be flashed upon it or a movie shown representing the answer to the question asked. Accept the *first* thought or answer that comes to you after asking the question, even if you judge it to make no sense or to be otherwise inappropriate. It may well be the answer in code. You can then work on decoding it.

28. Q. How do I deal with someone in my life who is always very negative to me?

A. Ask your Guide to take you to the image of that person in the inner world. Then ask that image to take its true form *as it exists as an energy in you.* Accept whatever form appears. If it turns into a green frog, work with the green frog. Ask what it needs from you to be healed *as an energy within you* (having nothing to do with the outer world person). Ask what it may have to give you that you're not accepting. Ask what part of you it represents. This 'true form' will represent the force that is projecting out of you onto that outer person and causing him or her to act negatively toward you. You will find that the outer person will either change or go out of your life when you heal the unconscious form you project on him or her. You will change the role need of the energy.

Say that your neighbour is trying to poison your dog. Ask your Guide to take you to or bring you the image of that neighbour as you know him to be in the outer world. Then give that image permission to take its true form as it lives in you. Say that it turns into Dracula. The Dracula image is a picture of the energy in you that projects out from you onto your neighbour and gets him to try to poison your dog. Call on the tarot *Sun* and *Fool*. Ask them to send their love into the figure to heal and transform it so that it reaches its highest possible form in you at this time. After they do this, say that the Dracula figure has turned into a King figure. Dracula and the King are the *same energy,* the King being its higher, more conscious form. Ask the King what *you* have to do new in thought, action or behaviour (having nothing to do with your neighbour), so that the energy he (the King) represents in you will remain constant and not sink back into unconsciousness and its Dracula form. When you have received this information, give the King energy form permission to enter your body. Feel what part of you this energy lives in and radiates from. If the transformation is successful and you have really changed this part of yourself, the neighbour will change dramatically or go out of your life immediately. Because you have changed your role needs and no longer need a dog poisoner in your reality, the neighbour's choices are to change as a role player for you or leave your reality.

Never work with images of known people from the outer world in the inner world. It tends to sustain rather than release projections. Always ask the known outer world person to take his true form as he lives as an energy within you. This insures that you are, in fact, working on an aspect of yourself. You can go to images of everyone you know and ask each of these outer world figures to take its true form as it lives in you. Here you will get the image of *what* you are projecting on each of them. It's both fascinating and revealing to do this and to discover just what we are projecting on those people we love best or least.

Healing of outer world people may not be done on the inner planes without their conscious ego consent. Interference, no matter how well intentioned, with the life of another *without that person's permission given verbally on the outer planes* is against the Law. Healing, all too often, turns into an ego power trip, so be sure to call or write the person to be healed for their permission for a healing from you. The only things we are allowed to send another without his or her permission is Love and Light.

29. Q. Money is a constant problem in my life. Which archetype would I see to work on this and make this area more conscious?

A. This would have to do, in terms of the horoscope, with factors relating to the Second House (the sign on the Cusp, a planet or planets in the House, the planet ruling the House, or the so-called 'hard angles' to any of these) and the archetypes of the Tarot *High Priest* or *Hierophant* (Taurus) and *The Empress* (Venus).

Problems in the money area are always connected to problems in three other areas of life: love, sex and life goals. If there is a problem in the Second House (money, resources, oral needs, income, food, supply), look also to the Fifth House (the personal love area, relations to children, self-expression, art, creativity, hobbies), the Eighth House (sex, regeneration, death, debt, metamorphosis, taxes, rebirth, astral projection, transformation, levitation, Kundalini), and to the Eleventh House (life goals measured by one's personal death, impersonal love, altruism, humanitarianism, friendship, groups you belong to – or don't belong to). A change in one will foster a change in all. Let your Inner Guide advise you where to focus.

30. Q. Will meditation help my lower back pain?

A. Lower back pain is a classic symptom of a partnership

problem. It has to do with the natural Libra area or Seventh House of the horoscope, which rules the lumbar region and the kidneys. It also has to do with the individual's Shadow – one's *other half* or *alter ego* which is always projected onto and manipulates the marriage or business partner, the room-mate, one's third sibling and one's second child. The Shadow figure exists within you as a constant partner and is always of the same sex as yourself. As the ego separated itself from the Great All between birth and seven years of age, the Shadow simultaneously formed on the inner planes to balance the ego and keep it from dissolving. As the ego became the 'I', the Shadow formed itself from the 'not-I' elements – everything the ego thought it was not or did not possess as negative or positive aspects of itself. The Shadow is both partner and balance to the ego. It must be confronted and made a conscious friend and companion before the ego can achieve stability with the Centre. *You and your Shadow are the two halves of one whole.*

I recommend asking the Guide to present your Shadow to you as one of the first steps in the Inner Guide Meditation. Ask the Shadow figure what it needs from you to start functioning as friend and conscious partner. Ask, if you were to give it part of one day of every week to do what it needs to do for its expression through you in your life, what would it like to do, where would it like to go? Give your other half expression compatible to you both. As you deal with your Shadow, lower back pain and all other Seventh House problems will begin to clear up.

31.   Q. I ask the archetypes to have certain things happen in the outer world. They say they will, but then the things don't happen. I feel that I'm putting myself on with the meditation. Why don't the promises of the archetypes come true?

A. You're experiencing what is called the 'Magic Mirror Effect'. When the ego is heavily invested in the results of outer world situations, it will only accept answers that coincide with its desires. (Think of the Wicked Queen and her magic mirror in *Snow White*). We always encounter this effect when we try to change outer reality without focusing on changing and becoming more conscious ourselves. If you approach the meditation asking for things, the 'Magic Mirror' will operate until the ego understands that all outer changes result from changes on deep inner levels. As you meditate more and allow the process to flow, you will find that your needs are filled without your having to ask.

A technique for helping to overcome the 'Magic Mirror Effect' that we have developed here at D.O.M.E. is to ask your Inner Guide to flash a *red light* if you are not getting truth and a *green light* if you are. It seems to be easier for us to create and manipulate words than it is to create or manipulate colours or images.

Perhaps instead of asking for certain things to occur, you might ask your Guide to take you to those parts of you that *prevent* things from changing or flowing in your outer life. You can then remove the blockages in your life flow and learn to co-create with the reality-generating energies.

32. Q. If you were to recommend only *one* question to ask and work on with the Inner Guide, what would that question be?

A. 'How do I wake up and become *all* of myself?'

33. Q. When I describe the Inner Guide Meditation, friends and acquaintances say that I am dabbling in black magic and the occult or put the meditation down in some way. What can I do about this?

A. Your friends and acquaintances are living out your own unconscious doubts and fears. Ask your Guide to take you to the figure or figures that are causing these doubts and fears. Work with them to bring them into conscious and useful forms, and you will find that your friends and acquaintances will change their attitudes. No amount of words will convince people of the truth of any spiritual practice. Only the example of your own life and being will demonstrate the validity of your path. The fruit of the tree is the proof of the tree.

Remember, our Saturn and Capricorn energies test us every inch of our way to make certain that we don't miss a step in our personal spiritual evolutions.

34.   Q. As I go along from meditation to meditation, my results seem to be less dramatic, less certain, less precise, slower. Why does this happen?

A. This could indicate that you're approaching an *ego death*, a period when the current ego will be assimilating a major energy which heretofore has been repressed, triggering a transformation of the ego. Often an ego death is preceded by a depression or by the symptoms you mention. Fear and resistance to change are what cause the experiences you have described. If you really discipline yourself at this point to meditate more, to give more permissions, to receive instructions on how to ease and facilitate the transition, to really *listen* and *be receptive* on the inner planes, you will find that the entire meditative experience clears and that the contact deepens with both the Guide and the archetypal energy forms.

35.   Q. What does the Inner Guide Meditation have to do with God?

A. As you work with and feel the inner forces you carry in their various forms, you will discover your connection to and understanding of what God (or the Great Spirit or All That Is or the Source of All, etc.) is all about in a very direct and individual way. The spiritual experiences that occur in the inner worlds are intense and personal. Realization that God exists and is not just a theoretical concept is overwhelming to most, especially to those whose reality is based on materialistic concepts and beliefs. The 22 energies that the tarot pictures symbolize are 22 different aspects of the God force. We are unable to experience the totality of God in one step – *Enoch walked with God and* was not. But as we experience these energies, we begin to evolve our own realization of God. This is probably why the first apparent result of the Inner Guide Meditation tends to be a dramatic change in the personal value system.

36.   Q. Do the Inner Guides ever function if you don't plug into them through meditation?

A. Yes. The Guides function from birth. Many people experience the Guide when in mortal danger, before a possible car accident, for instance. They might hear a voice out of the air say, 'Stop!' 'Turn to the right' or 'Take your hands off the steering wheel'. Many times the answers that we receive when we pray for help come through the Guides. The Guide is the inner teacher who seems to have the job of trying to keep us alive on the planet so that we can accomplish what we came here to do. He leads us toward whatever personal realization of God we can accept. One of the characteristics of the Guide is that he doesn't judge or flatter or volunteer anything. He's just sort of *there*. The only times I've heard of Guides interfering within the meditation context or out in life were in cases of physical danger or when there was danger of the psyche being overwhelmed by the archetypal energies. In these latter situations the Guide will act spontaneously to pull you beyond the influence of the energy.

37. Q. Are the Inner Guides ever known figures from this life?

A. No. Never accept as your Guide a figure, either living or dead, that you have known or known of previously in life. The Guide is not a person who was alive when you took your first breath on the planet.

You might find that people whose Rising Sign corresponds to the sign on the Cusp of the Ninth House in your horoscope or whose Sun is in the sign that is on your Ninth House Cusp will automatically take the projection of your Guide's energy. But that outer person is *not* your Guide. If a known person does appear, look past him to your right and your inner world Guide will be there. The Guides are always within us during our lifetime, not outside of us.

38. Q. I have heard you say: 'To know how you are doing, just look around you'. What do you mean by this?

A. Forces that are literally being projected *through* each individual create the reality or holographic universe that each individual experiences. This is the process that a horoscope describes. Thus, *whatever* is in your world is not there by accident. *There are no chance happenings or coincidences. Your* energies are completely responsible for *everything* that is going on around you. If you see two people suddenly get into an argument in a restaurant, though it may appear to have nothing to do with you, an inspection of your horoscope would reveal that a Mars vibration is being activated in your particular pattern. It's in the nature of a warning to you, the ego, to work on the developing problem before it moves closer. Many people think that taking responsibility for the total environment is a *blame trip*, but this is not so. We are truly responsible for the outer dream, but not to blame for it any more than we are to blame for the inner dream. We develop only as rapidly as we can accomplish the necessary psychological and physical changes. But, if you accept responsibility for what is happening in your world, then you can *do* something to change it in yourself. If you separate from your reality experience by thinking of it as unconnected to you, then there is nothing you can do to improve it.

If a negative event is occurring anywhere in your world, ask the Guide to take you to that part of you that is either causing it or connected to it. Accept as correct whichever figure the Guide presents to you. It may not be one of the tarot archetypes. Find out what the figure needs from you to heal the negative situation in your outer world. Also, ask what it might be trying to communicate to you that the ego is not accepting.

And remember, taking either credit or blame for outer world situations is pure ego arrogance.

39.   Q. Where am I when I'm working with the Inner Guide?

A. It seems that meditating with the Guide is a way of altering the level of consciousness so that we are *awake* on the reality level immediately adjacent to and primary to our own, the level where dreams take place. That's why meditations have the tendency of slipping back into the unconscious if not written down, in the same way that dreams often do. Fifteen minutes after returning from contact with the Guide and the inner world forms you might begin to lose details. An hour later you may lose the entire experience, unless you write it down in your journal. The reality level on which we work with our

Guides seems to be *primary* to the outer world reality level. It *produces* the experience that we call reality, therefore changes made on the inner level rapidly change our outer worlds. We seem to have been taught everything exactly backwards. That which our culture calls 'just the imagination' actually is the level that creates our outer experience. We get lost in the outer world *symptoms* and ignore their *causes* on the inner planes, closer to the Source of All.

'I don't have time to meditate' or 'I'm too busy to meditate' are thoughts that keep us locked at the symptom level and powerless to effect change until the pain of our unconsciousness prods us in some way.

40.   Q. How do you regard pain?

A. Pain is a warning. Whenever we are feeling pain on *any* level, physical, emotional, mental or spiritual, it is an indication that we are out of or moving away from our own Centres. There is no pain when one is moving *toward* the Self. Pain is one of our safety sensations that tells us that something major is wrong. Sometimes it's the only way the Self can get us to stop and listen.

41.   Q. How can I know which archetypes to work with?

A. The easiest way to determine which archetypes to work with is to have your horoscope calculated with an Astrology-Tarot Equivalent Worksheet that translates the horoscope into tarot image terms. This presents the *bones* of your reality-generating energy system. This Worksheet may be obtained from D.O.M.E. in Colorado Springs, Colorado (see back of book).

42.   Q. I find that the tarot pictures bring forth an immediate identification with fortune telling, black magic and the like. I find them not relevant to me. They seem to impede my progress with the Guide.

A. If you have this difficulty, don't use them. Trust the Inner Guide. Your own unconscious will present these archetypal energies in the forms they take within you. I utilize the tarot images because they are the most convenient and accessible forms for translating a horoscopic pattern into images that an individual can use immediately. The archetypes, as they are encountered on the inner planes, seldom resemble the images on the tarot cards. The Tarot *Old Pan*, for instance, may present itself as a man in a business suit or the Tarot *High Priestess*, a grandmother figure. At any rate, they will change and evolve no matter what forms they initially take or what images you initially choose to use.

43.   Q. What are the dangers of working inside?

A. There is no danger as long as you're with the true Inner Guide, but it can be extremely dangerous to work with the archetypes without the Guide. The Guide will not allow you to touch more of the inner energies than you are able to physically and psychologically absorb. Because of my enthusiasm when I first discovered the Guide, I would ask to work with ten or twelve of the archetypes in one meditation. The Guide would seem to go along with this, but then, after we worked with three or four of the energy forms, he would say, 'That's enough for now', and would return me to our meeting place. The Guide is the one to trust in knowing whether or not you are interacting with the archetypes too much. If such is the case, he may suggest just sitting and talking with him or resting and getting calm on the inner plane.

Many people also say that, on occasion, they lost their Guides. This generally happens when one resists the inner process. The person goes *looking* for the Guide to no avail. In this instance it is better just to *call* him. He will be there. Once you've touched the Guide, you will find it difficult to lose him. He's with you for life and possibly thereafter. You may feel his presence often during the course of your daily life.

Don't forget how dangerous it can be to work in the unconscious without your Guide. The archetypes are your reality makers. They are extremely powerful energies, and they can literally blow your circuits or cause death if your Guide isn't there to serve as buffer and gauge of their energies. For example, about three years after I had begun working with the Guide, my cat developed an abscess behind one of her eyes. Since, in my particular horoscopic pattern, the Tarot *Empress* has to do with pets, I asked the Guide to take me to *The Empress* form and asked her what I had to give in return for this healing. I was told what I had to do, the Guide OKed it, and I agreed to do what she asked. *The Empress* agreed to heal the cat. I completed the requested task, but after two days, I could see no change in the animal's condition. This time in meditation I went directly to *The Empress* without calling the Guide (rationalizing that I had already worked on this problem while he was present and not wanting to bother him about it again). *The Empress* said, 'She's healing'. I pointed out that, since I had immediately kept my part of the bargain, I thought it only fair that the cat be healed by the next morning. *The Empress* replied that she would do this, and I returned from the meditation satisfied.

However, after going to bed, I awoke during the night perspiring so profusely that it seemed I had lost gallons of water from my system and was continuing to lose more. The next morning I found that the cat's abscess had broken and healed, but I was so weak that I thought *I* was going to die. I immediately went to the Guide. He said that I had been foolish to work with energies I didn't really understand without his presence. Without his being there to set up safeguards, the experience could have caused me serious damage if the animal had been a little more ill. He said the healing energy of the Tarot *Empress* had to go through me, the physical vehicle, to heal the cat.

That was the last time I worked in the inner world without the Guide.

44. Q. Do you regard yourself as higher or spiritually better than other people because you are working with your Inner Guide?

A. When, through practice, you understand the philosophical and spiritual implications underlying the Inner Guide Meditation, you will see that everyone you experience is a projection of a combination of your own energies. Since you have all possibilities within you, those you experience are aspects of yourself. This is a humbling and unifying realization. You won't be able to put yourself on by looking in the mirror and saying, 'Boy, have I got it together', when your Uncle Jim's health is breaking down, for instance. Uncle Jim is an aspect of you, a reflection of your internal energies. Thus, if he is in bad shape, so is some inner part of you that he corresponds to. All the people in our lives correspond in this way to inner aspects of ourselves. In a Universe of Oneness, who can be higher or better than any other? We just have different jobs to do.

45.   Q. Do you think you have come up with 'the' spiritual answer for contemporary Western man?

A. I've spent my lifetime looking for tools for evolving spiritual consciousness. This one continually works, bringing positive results and life changes. It is not a fragile method and can endure the sceptical testing of Western man and woman. It is an active method involving doing, image-making, question asking. It begins with an emphasis on the use of the senses and on stabilizing the physical plane, and it progresses according to each individual's needs. Any path that moves one toward his or her own experience and realization of God holds 'the' spiritual answer for the person utilizing it.

46.   Q. Are you against Eastern spiritual practices?

A. I feel that Western methods work best for Westerners, and that we are born in a certain geographical place for good karmic reasons. But, of course, the test of any spiritual practice is in the life results it produces. If you see the members of your family and those around you getting healthier and more conscious coincident to your spiritual practice, you will know that the practice is *working* both inside and out. If you don't see these changes happening in your life, you might seriously question your current spiritual path.

Three years in the Orient demonstrated to me the need of the West to get its spiritual tools back, tools hidden, lost or destroyed because of the severe suppression practiced for centuries by the Western religious establishment. The tools of the East are useful and beautiful, but we need to get the rust off of our own and to rediscover those we had.

However, I'm for any method that will enable us to get to God. Whichever spiritual path works for you is the one you should be on. But *stick to it*. Most delays and detours in one's spiritual evolution are the results of 'trip tasting' – bouncing from one spiritual trip to the next and gaining the rewards of none of them.

47. Q. How important is the horoscope in terms of the Inner Guide Meditation?

A. I find it invaluable because the horoscope tells which energies are in conflict or polarized and which forces can be utilized to help resolve the problems. Working in terms of a horoscope that has been translated into tarot image terms gives you a way to re-wire yourself, in a sense. You can zero in on problems that may have remained hidden for years in a psychiatric context. Many psychiatrists and psychologists, especially the Jungians and the younger therapists, use astrology as a time-saving tool. By working with your own archetypal energy pattern you are working at the *core* of your reality-creating, reality-sustaining mechanism.

48. Q. What can I do when I can't seem to stop blaming someone for something they've done to me? My mind is willing to stop it, but my feelings won't.

A. What I recommend in this instance is changing the thought from 'Look at what they've done to me' to 'Look at what *my* energies have made them do to me'. If you make this change in your thinking pattern, you should notice a corresponding change in your feelings. Seek out the energy form within yourself that manipulates the outer person or persons, and heal it within yourself.

49. Q. Why do you use the words 'parts' to refer to the people in our lives?

A. A part is a piece of a whole. I use the word 'part' to remind myself and others that any person or thing that appears to be separate from ourselves is actually an aspect of the greater whole.

50.   Q. Dark menacing figures block the exit from the cave
into the landscape when I attempt the Inner Guide
Meditation. What should I do?

A. Occasionally an ego's resistance to change will put
blocks in the way to the Guide in the forms of walls,
snakes, a beast standing in our way or unknown figures
attempting to distract us from the goal of contacting the
Guide. **IGNORE THESE.** Walk through the things in
your path, and you will find they dissolve. Disregard the
people or entities who try to distract you from meeting
the Inner Guide. There is no possible danger until you
are beyond the place where you first meet the Guide. Just
follow the animal to your Guide. Beyond the meeting
place, the Guide remains with you as teacher, friend and
protector.

51.   Q. With your world philosophy, do you take responsibility
for the actions of the President of the country?

A. Yes. This has to do with what I call the 'Seven Circles of
Movement'. Our reality tends to give us messages that
move toward us through a sequence of seven circles.
First, we read a newspaper account of an event happening
in a foreign country. Then, we hear about its happening
in our country. Then, we hear about its happening in our
state, then in our city, then to an acquaintance and then
to a friend or family member. If we're not getting the
message by this time, something will happen to the ego
itself.

When a problem is healed or transformed within, it
moves away in these same seven circles, but as a
succession of *resolved* problems that you hear about in
various ways. This means that the President of the
country does give us a message of what's happening
inside of ourselves. We can go to the force within that
corresponds to the outer world President. If we keep that
part of ourselves healed, it will help him in the outer
world.

52.   Q. What do you think about death?

A. I think that death as we now understand it will last
perhaps another ten years or less. We are just becoming

aware that more than one 'body' constitutes a human being. Acupuncture makes us aware of this second body, as does Kirlian photography, and medicine is starting to recognize that there are two bodies, not one, to be dealt with. It may soon recognize that there are more than two.

More and more out-of-body experiences are being acknowledged and reported. People are beginning to discuss more openly these astral projection experiences. If you have projected astrally, you already know what death is like. It is just like astral projection, but without the ability to re-enter the physical body.

Death is another of our favourite illusions. As we become more aware of who we are and what we carry, the experience of death and the attitude toward it will change dramatically. If you have ever been out-of-body or have had a temporary death experience, you already know that death is not an ending. If the experience isn't beautiful, you haven't died!

I would refer anyone interested in this subject to the book by Dr Raymond A. Moody, Jr., *Life After Life* and the work of Dr Elisabeth Kübler-Ross, the 'death and dying lady'.

53. Q. My Inner Guide has approved when archetypes have requested behaviour that is highly frowned upon by society or my friends or peers. Why is this?

A. The true Guide will encourage *whatever* is necessary or useful for an individual's growth and evolution, often despite current social values. Of course, this can be painful for an ego until it adjusts to a new view of society and its structures and rules. I've never known a true Guide to encourage or approve of anything that would harm another person in any way or interfere with another's freedom or evolution. Nor have I heard of a Guide encouraging anything that would be destructive to the individual's spiritual growth. Remember that society's values are ephemeral and often conflict with eternal truths.

54. Q. How do I know that results from the Inner Guide Meditation aren't just coincidence?

A. At first, when the Inner Guide Meditation moves beyond theory into experience, the results may seem coincidental. After a while, however, they go beyond coincidence, because the number of coincidences becomes too overwhelming. We then begin to experience the fact that changes in our environments correspond directly to our inner work. This is often shocking to the rational system of the ego, because it must develop a new view of how reality works, one which supersedes the established materialistic view.

55.   Q. Why don't I *want* to meditate?

A. When large-scale changes in a personality occur, it is frequently threatening to the current ego. We become habituated to certain opinions and types of behaviour. Just as conservative factions develop out in the world to slow down social and political changes, so do elements of the ego with vested interests in a certain manner of being try to prevent changes in these areas. Even when we eventually learn that the changes are beneficial, we unconsciously and automatically do this. For most, it is frightening to move into the unknown.

Defenses against changes that develop take the form of being 'too busy to meditate', feeling that 'this doesn't work for me' or taking a 'Who cares?' attitude about inner work.

Interestingly enough, it's when the changes and growth *do* start that many people say 'this doesn't work' and go off to find another spiritual path which they remain on until *that* path begins to change them, and so on, *ad infinitum,* or until they become aware of the game they are playing with themselves.

56.   Q. What about the Third House guide? Is it always 'bad' or 'evil'?

A. Not at all. It seems that the Third House guide serves to maintain the ego's stability. This guide seems to represent the rationalization system of the mind. Many people work with the Ninth and the Third House entities together. This seems to work fine as long as the Ninth House Guide's primacy is not usurped.

The Third House guides seem to have no ability to protect us in the inner worlds. However, if a male or female Third House guide shows up, trust your true Guide. If he says it is alright that he comes along and you would like him to, it's often a good working arrangement.

57. Q. I get very strange physical sensations when I work with some of the archetypes, especially when I ask the Guide to bring two or more together to touch each other and me or when I make a circle of hands with a group of them and my Guide. What causes this?

A. Remember that the energy forms you are interacting with are those potent energies that create and sustain your personal reality. What I call 'The Alice phenomena' (from *Alice in Wonderland*) are common experiences in the Inner Guide Meditation. These are feelings of shrinking, falling, expanding physically and of extreme weight or weightlessness that usually take place in the presence of the archetypal energy forms.

Activation of the Kundalini energy or Serpent Power which 'sleeps' at the base of the spine, with its attendant sensation of heat, cold or electricity shooting up the spine or up from the feet, is also a side effect of this meditation and necessitates the presence and supervision of the Inner Guide to insure the safety of the experience.

58. Q. How do marijuana and alcohol affect the Inner Guide Meditation and the rest of the life?

A. Marijuana effectively blocks initial contact with the true Inner Guide for up to ten days following its use. It affects the ego in such a way that those unconscious elements that presently control or manipulate the ego are further distorted or blocked from being understood, allowing inflation of the ego and increased separation from the heart centre, one's true nature. The fear mechanism that strives to keep the current ego from growing and changing is strengthened by marijuana, its derivatives, and by alcohol. Alcohol and marijuana are the two drugs which pull us into the unconscious Collective Mind or Mass Mind, the mind that fosters and perpetuates the illusions of separation and non-unity, and attempts at all costs to maintain the *status quo*, the mind of mediocrity. They keep us internally and externally bound to and dependent on the unconscious mother-father (Moon-Saturn, Cancer-Capricorn) archetypes and away from the development of our own freedom, creativity and individuality.

In astrological terms, alcohol suppresses the Lunar (Tarot *High Priestess*) and the Cancerian (Tarot *Chariot*) energies in the reality-generating system, while marijuana suppresses the energies of Saturn (Tarot *World*) and Capricorn (Tarot *Old Pan* or *Devil*). This can be demonstrated through an individual's horoscope. Of those people related to you through blood, law or role, the ones that correspond to the astrological Houses containing your Moon and Cancer energies, will suffer in their lives or create problems in your life as you use alcohol, and the ones that correspond to the Houses containing the Saturn and Capricorn energies, will suffer or cause problems for you as you use marijuana. This includes the Fourth House of the horoscope, the natural House of Cancer – mother, home, emotional base, family as a unit, security, father's third sibling, as being responsive negatively to alcohol, and the Tenth House, the natural House of Capricorn – father, employer, authority figures, policemen, reputation, honour, public success, 'the powers that be', the Establishment, mother's third sibling, as being negatively responsive to marijuana.

Marijuana seems to be the more insidious of the two drugs, because it is a drug that 'lies' to the individual, telling the person's ego that his or her abilities to love and create are becoming greater, when, in fact, it rips off these abilities and replaces them with the *illusion* of having these increased abilities, and then usually defends the illusion with a paranoid ego stance – 'I'm right, and they're wrong', 'Nobody really understands', 'I'm surrounded by enemies' (usually non-marijuana users) and the like.

If you regard the Cancer-Capricorn pole of a horoscope as a seesaw, marijuana smoking suppresses the Capricorn end resulting in the Cancerian end raising too high and becoming unbalanced – the emotions go out of control, the personality becomes grandiose, all limits dissolve into the boundless, and the ego goes into a manic phase, often quite severe. If a physician is consulted, he will often prescribe some mood balancing drug, through ignorance of the mechanics of the four-body system. This results first in stabilization, but then in increased desire or need for the marijuana, which in turn produces depression, paranoia, exhaustion, fear and guilt. Thus a classical manic-depressive syndrome is created and maintained until both drugs, the marijuana and the mood stabilizer, have been dispensed with and the four-body system returns to its own balance. This is the seesaw effect often observed in marijuana users. It takes away the individual's abilities to love and create – to do the work of his or her own heart centre. It makes invisible to the ego the true purpose of the life, and it injures all those around the person, generally those who love the person most and are the closest (family, friends).

It is a tragedy of our time that alcohol and marijuana are so poorly understood. Perhaps with the advent of the dawning Aquarian Age, the fears that motivate their usage will dissolve. In a time of vast changes on all the levels of reality – the time we now live in – fear of change becomes prominent. Only meditation – some form of going within – effectively deals with these fears.

59.   Q. Are there other test questions to ask the Inner Guide?

A. One that has been suggested is, 'Is your life dedicated to the cause of total truthfulness?'

60.   Q. What are the reasons for the Guides communicating with us?

A. From what many Inner Guides have said, I gather that their help and teaching is part of their own further evolution. For a more specific answer to this question, ask your Guide.

61.   Q. Now when I begin to meditate, as soon as I close my eyes I find myself with the Guide on the archetypal level. Is it all right to not go through the procedure of cave, landscape, animal, etc.?

A. This phenomenon occurs in most people after they

XII.

HANGED MAN

Trump of *The Hanged Man* from the Jerry Kay *Book of Thoth* Tarot Deck.

have been meditating for a while. It seems to indicate that the ego has learned to instantaneously transfer itself to the level where the Guide and the archetypes live without need for the previous structure. If your Guide approves, it's all right.

62. Q. What does it mean when archetypes change form dramatically, especially after months or years of being in the same form?

A. This usually indicates a major breakthrough in the area that archetype has to do with in outer and inner life. It is generally verified by people in your outer world commenting that you have 'changed' in some respect, or you yourself noticing that an entire area of your reality experience has altered.

63. Q. I see people in my outer world who seem to have it all together who don't have any interest in spiritual or inner work. They seem happy and have good jobs and family lives. Why can't I get it together as easily as they do?

A. We can never be sure what is going on in another person's reality experience. All we can know is what we experience of our own energies projected onto the screens of others. What you see in those people are those parts of yourself that *are* together within you. As you come more into Centre, you will find more 'together' people in the world around you.

64. Q. A friend of mine has been working with the Inner Guide Meditation for only a month, and she is already working with her fourth Guide. How can I get to my other Guides faster?

A. Because of the slowness of the physical body in changing, I would suspect that your friend may be experiencing a procession of false guides. We reach the second Guide only after the physical vehicle has changed enough to handle more intense vibrational energy. This often takes years. Observe what your friend reports about her outer life, what the fruit of her tree has truly been. At any rate, spiritual progress is not a foot race. *Which* Guide one is working with has little to do with one's spiritual progress or evolution. Someone working with the third Guide might well be further from Centre than someone working with the first. There is no hurry. We have all the time we need for our own evolution. When we miss steps, we often get a severe message from our own lives or from the lives of those close to us that this is the case. See what her life's events have been trying to tell your friend.

65. Q. My Guide predicted the death of a friend and it didn't happen. Why?

A. True Guides do not make predictions, especially about other people and their lives.

66. Q. I asked my Inner Guide the date of my death and could not get a clear answer. Doesn't he know?

A. A death date could only be given based on the assumption that you would stay exactly where you are in your evolution without further change or awareness. The very fact you are working with the Guide in the inner dimensions will change the state of your unconsciousness to some degree. We are only predictable if nothing in our interior systems changes.

Astrologically we go through many death cycles during the course of one lifetime. The horoscopic factors that indicate a physical death and a spiritual rebirth are the same. We die physically when the ego no longer is able to serve the Centre and the Centre withdraws. According to the horoscope, death or rebirth usually correspond to the simultaneous activation of the First, Fourth and Eighth Houses of the natal pattern.

67. Q. What tarot cards correpond to the planets beyond Pluto or within Mercury's orbit? I'm referring to the planets Vulcan, Trans-Pluto, Psyche, Lilith and other invisible planets I have heard astrologers refer to.

A. Until these 'planets' appear on the physical plane of our Universe, I recommend ignoring them. I have *never* found any event which was not explained by the action of one of the eight known planets or the sun or moon. These 'invisible planets' (or 'moons') only have the power you invest them with in your thinking until they become manifest in the Universe, as Pluto, our last planet, did in 1930. Discuss this question with your Inner Guide and ask his opinion.

68. Q. You use the term 'Alien' in describing some horoscopes. What do you mean by this, where do Aliens come from, and what is the responsibility of an Alien this lifetime?

A. The teaching about the Aliens (which I received in a dream, November 8, 1974) is explained in a later section: 'How to Translate a Horoscope into Tarot Terms for a Worksheet'. As to *where* an Alien comes from, I don't know, nor do I regard it as important. I use the term to describe the subjective feelings that the possessors of certain horoscopic patterns experience. An Alien pattern contains highly specialized talents and abilities, usually of an ESP or other paranormal variety – the kind of talent or ability which would get one burned as a witch or a warlock some centuries back. The responsibility of an Alien is the same as for anyone: to awaken to himself and bring his gifts into consciousness for the service of humanity. (All the Aliens seem to have begun 'waking up' since November 21, 1974, when the planet Uranus went into the sign Scorpio.)

There seems to be a consistent pattern in life which all the Aliens experience. Their powers are accepted and taken for granted by themselves (although not necessarily by their families) until they first encounter their peer group at about seven years of age. They frighten their peers or are thought of and reacted to as strange, weird or different, and their peers reject them. The Alien usually reacts with 'There's something wrong with me' and begins to regard his talents as 'bad' aspects of himself. The suppression of these talents begins as he learns to 'fake it' out in the world, to appear 'like everybody else', to pass for 'normal' in human society. (The first seven years of an Alien's life are generally locked away from memory.) This 'faking it' process is usually successful, but the sense of alienation remains acute. There is often a period of extreme depression or of suicidal feelings or attempts in the late teens or early twenties, and we lose many Aliens during this time if the Alien is not recognized and helped by another Alien or someone with insight into the actual problem.

The awakening, which began in 1974, has not been easy. When a person has been suppressing something since seven years of age, he doesn't rush to embrace it. A number of steps are necessary. The Inner Guides ease the re-acceptance of the Alien components and allow their re-assimilation into the life in as non-jarring a way as possible.

69.   Q. Because of the connection to astrology and the tarot, is the Inner Guide Meditation anti-Christian?

A. Jesus taught: 'In my Father's house are many mansions'. Ask your Guide to take you to meet and talk with Jesus about this and any other questions you have about the role of Christ and the teachings of the Bible and of the Christian churches. Many priests, brothers and ministers are beginning to utilize the Inner Guide Meditation for themselves and in pastoral care. Love and truth are never threats to true spiritual practice.

The Magi or Wise Men from the East in the biblical story of Jesus were astrologers. As the late Moby Dick, an astrologer from Honolulu, Hawaii, put it, 'Wise men follow the stars'.

70.   Q. My wife and I both have Worksheets with the astrological factors translated into tarot terms. Should we also have our horoscopes compared to see how they affect one another?

A. To me, horoscope comparison (comparing the astrological factors in another or making a 'composite chart') does little to decrease unconscious projection between two people. In fact, it seems to do the reverse. Your wife's role in your reality experience is *totally* described in *your* pattern. She lives out *your* Shadow side. The comparison of your charts would further increase the illusion of separation.

71.   Q. Is the Inner Guide an aspect of my ego?

A. No. The Guides do not always cater to our ego whims and fancies. They say and do what is needed, not wanted.

They know our limits and our inadequacies and allow exposure to unconscious materials which the ego itself would never choose to deal with.

72.   Q. Why is it easy for some people to contact the Inner Guide and difficult for others?

A. The individual make-up determines the ease or difficulty of the contact, as does the ego's motivation to change, grow and expand beyond current limits. Feeling based, non-cerebral individuals seem to have the easiest time with the Guide contact, as do those with a strong psychic or mystic bent and creative artists. Paranoid personality types, users of drugs, intellectuals and analytical types often have the most difficulty at first.

73.   Q. Is my Shadow described in my horoscope?

A. Yes. The horoscope of your Shadow side is *your horoscope upside-down*. The Descendant of your horoscope (the Cusp or beginning of the Seventh House) is your Shadow's *Ascendant* or Rising Sign. The Shadow contains all the astrological energies that the ego represses and thinks it does not possess, both positive and negative. Our Shadow figures are always of the same sex as we are, a male having a male Shadow.

74.   Q. What is the difference between how I use my imagination in day-dreaming and how it is used in the Inner Guide Meditation?

A. Dr Carl G. Jung answers this question in his book, *Psychological Types*, written in 1921:
   'We can distinguish between *active* and *passive* fantasy. *Active* fantasies are the product of intuition; i.e., they are evoked by an attitude directed to the perception of unconscious contents, as a result of which the libido immediately invests all the elements emerging from the unconscious and, by association with parallel material, brings them into clear focus in visual form.
   'Passive fantasies always have their origin in an unconscious process that is antithetical to consciousness, but invested with approximately the same amount of energy as the conscious attitude, and therefore

capable of breaking through the latter's resistance. Active fantasies, on the other hand, owe their existence not so much to this unconscious process as to a conscious propensity to assimilate hints or fragments of lightly-toned elements, to elaborate them in clearly visual form. It is not necessarily a question of a dissociated psychic state, but rather of a positive participation of consciousness.

'Active fantasy is one of the highest forms of psychic activity. For here the conscious mind and the unconscious personality of the subject flow together into a common product in which both are united.'[1]

75.   Q. How do I change my outer world more quickly? I keep working with my Guide to change things, but the negative people in my life seem to never change.

A. The first step toward reality change is *acceptance*, without judgement, of the way things are – the way *you* are. The goal of the Inner Guide Meditation is not to change other people or to change the outer world. It is to evolve oneself spiritually through increased awareness of oneself and the energies one carries. To focus on outer change is to block our flow through involvement with *symptoms* instead of *causes*. The 'negative people' are there to show you *your* resistance to change. To keep focused on negativity *feeds* that negativity. Don't worry about those other people. Focus on yourself. They change when your creation energies no longer require them to show you certain aspects of your own consciousness.

76.   Q. You speak of the 'Law of No'. Would you explain this?

A. What we say 'No' to in life literally structures our realities, both inside and out. The *absolute* No's, 'Thou shalt not . . .' 'Under no circumstances would I ever . . .', give form to the walls, floors and ceilings of our reality boxes. The *qualified* No's, 'Usually I wouldn't do this, but . . .' and our 'Maybe's', are the doors and windows of our reality boxes. To change an absolute No to a qualified No, a qualified No to a Yes, or to invent a new absolute or qualified No, literally changes one's inner and outer realities.

To discover what the No's are in your life, start making two lists of the things you say 'No' to; one list of the absolute No's, the other of the qualified No's. Every time you feel anxious, guilty, depressed, uptight or a 'should' comes into your mind, one of your No's is activated. Try to find out just what it is you're saying 'No' to, and whose No pattern you're obeying or reacting to.

The No's of the physical body, for instance, are the bones and the skin. They are useful to the body by giving it form and limit, so that it doesn't spill out as a boundless amoeba.

Measure your No's by their *usefulness* to your spiritual life, growth and evolution, not by whether they are 'right' or 'wrong'. Perhaps you've outgrown some of your No's. Perhaps you don't have enough No's for structure in your life, and chaos reigns. 'No' serves to give form and structure, but it becomes destructive when it begins to box in or strait-jacket life. Examine your pattern of No's honestly, and see if they truly serve *all* of you.

When we change one of our No's or invent a new No, we experience a testing process from outer life. You've probably experienced this if you've ever gone on a diet or tried to break a long-standing habit. It seems that suddenly everyone around you is conspiring to get you to eat something that's not on your diet or to fall back into the old habit in some way. This represents your own testing energies (the Moon, Saturn, Cancer and Capricorn in astrology) *making sure that you really mean it.* It's their job to maintain a stable structural reality for you, so, when they hear of a change in your present structure or rule system, they bring to you those individuals or situations in your outer reality which will function as your testers.

The time pattern of the testing process seems to be: almost daily for two weeks, then at least once a week, and then once a month until the new structure is secure and solid.

77. Q. I don't get the magical results in my life that others report. Why is this?

A. Much would depend on how you define 'magical'. Two hundred years ago flicking a switch and having electric lights come on would have been regarded as magic. We now understand this as physics.

A colleague of mine, John Woodsmall from Houston, Texas, reported that one of the people he worked with had this same complaint. She had worked on a stubborn health problem and complained that she had found no results on this from her inner work. My friend asked her how the health condition was. She replied that she had 'accidentally' run into a doctor at a party who knew exactly what was causing the problem, and that he had it cured in a week.

Because so-called results happen in our everyday worlds in everyday ways without rays coming down from Heaven, we tend to think of them as coincidence and do not relate them to our inner work. There is no predicting how 'results' will occur. I, the current ego, may think of six or seven ways a problem in my life might be solved. The energies within have an infinity of ways to cause things to happen. If we see, in truth, that our whole reality is magical, the surrender to our own Centres becomes easier, and all life becomes richer and more awesome.

78.   Q. What exactly is depression?

A. As I understand it, it is much the same as a depression in the earth. Something within the earth causes soil to sink in or down. We, too, are pulled in or down by a depression, but, generally, we don't think to turn around and face its cause. We look to the outer world for reasons and solutions. If you ask the Guide to take you to the cause of a depression, a figure or thing you can interact with, you can find both cause and cure quite rapidly. The cause is *never* outside, only the symptoms are.

79.   Q. What is a good cure for 'spaciness'?

A. Neptune, *The Hanged Man*, and Pisces, *The Moon* in tarot, are the archetypal energies having to do with spaciness. Working with these energies in meditation is one good way to deal with the problem. A walking-around-in-life cure seems to be to feel *all* of yourself in your feet. Feel what the ground feels like under your feet. Feel what your shoes feel like, what the bones in your feet feel like. Feel your weight on your feet. This exercise seems to bring all four of the bodies together and ends the feeling of spaciness by insistence that your feelings plug into your physical body.

80.   Q. What tarot archetypes are involved in the life crisis that often occurs after someone begins meditating and moving towards Centre?

A. The Tarot *Tower* and the Tarot *Devil* or *Old Pan* (Mars and Capricorn, in astrology) are pictures of the energies involved. The crisis involves an ego experience of great isolation, often coinciding with outer life trauma or extreme change on the physical, emotional, mental and/or spiritual planes. (This crisis is produced by any spiritual system that is designed to unite one with one's Center, rather than just produce a pleasant, harmonious life plateau.) If the crisis is passed successfully, the individual is then able to function in vertical polarity with his spiritual forces and in **horizontal polarity** with his outer world relations. If he fails this spiritual passage or point of crisis, he usually stops pushing further into spiritual work for the time being, and returns rapidly to the psychological condition he was in prior to meditating and working with the Guide on the inner planes. Because of the moth to flame pull of our spiritual natures, many of us face the crisis point again and again until a breakthrough is finally achieved. The biblical story of Job is a good example of the process.

81.   Q. When I am with a person of the opposite sex whom I am in love with, just *who* is that person in my movie? What aspect of myself is he, and what role am I playing?

A. Generally, in this situation, you, the woman, will be living out your own feminine energies (akin to Jung's concept of the *anima*), and the man you are in love with will be acting out, through projection, your masculine energies (Jung's concept of the *animus*). The 'I' we speak of is almost always the current ego, in this case allowing certain energies to flow *into* it, projecting others *through* itself onto the man.

82.   Q. Doesn't meditation encourage passivity to real world problems and actions?

A. I find that the contrary is true. Meditation during part of one's day doesn't cause withdrawal from the rest of life's activities. The archetypal energies frequently make recommendations concerning outer world actions. Also, meditation resolves the hang-ups and attachments to the outer world that prevent the individual from becoming himself freely and fully. This enables him to cope much more effectively with the outer world and the problems he encounters in it.

The Inner Guide Meditation does not encourage passivity to the problems of the outer world at large, but rather suggests that an individual is responsible for dealing with all the inner problems of which these outer problems and reactions are symptomatic. Working on these problems within tends to heal these outer world situations without the fruitless strife caused by isolating certain people, groups or political units outside of oneself and labelling them as the 'bad guys'. Fighting them violently or directly tends to make them stronger and more unconscious.

83.   Q. Sometimes I seem to go into a trance when I'm working with the Inner Guide and the archetypes. Is this all right?

A. No. We are too close to the vibration of the Aquarian Age for trance or mediumistic states to be safe for us (if they ever were). The Inner Guide Meditation requires full ego consciousness and participation. Ask your Guide to take you to the archetypal energy form that is causing this problem, and resolve it. Meditation is not a trance or hypnotic state. It is absolutely imperative that you, the ego, stay totally awake and self-aware in the meditation state.

84.   Q. Are we in the Aquarian Age?

A. No, I don't believe so. In his two books, *Beneath the Moon and Under the Sun* and *Lord of the Dawn, Quetzalcoatl,* Tony Shearer gives the only date for the beginning of the Aquarian Age to which I've ever had a gut level, *'That's it!'* response: **August 17, 1987**, the day that the so-called 'Aztec Calendar' ends. We'll see. Aquarius rules the element of surprise and the unexpected, as well as electricity and the Kundalini energy in humankind. Perhaps the Kundalini latent at the base of everyone's spine will rise simultaneously in each person on the planet. That would certainly fill the bill for the world ending in fire – the holy fire of Kundalini, the Serpent Power of God.

Kundalini activation seems to have already begun in many sensitive people, and instances of the awakening of this energy on a larger scale will probably be occurring in the early 1980's. It is the energy that will push humanity into its next evolutionary step as a transformed being.

85. Q. In brief, can you define what the tarot trumps are?

A. I consider them as 22 aspects of the energy I call God. They represent a way to experience individual aspects of the God-energy without blowing all the circuits. Remember, 'Enoch walked with God and was not'. The tarot archetypes are a way to *begin* touching intense spiritual energies – a way to develop *spiritual muscle*, so to speak.

One way I like to think about it is to imagine God as a 22 faceted jewel. *The Emperor*, then, can be thought of as a red facet, *The Empress* as a green facet, etc. Each of us sees only a partial grouping of facets, those facing us. But we're still all talking about the same thing, the One.

86. Q. Can you give a one-sentence definition of a horoscope?

A. A horoscope is a symbolic diagram which describes one person's entire universe from that one person's point of view.

87. Q. I know that the symbol for the Piscean Age is The Fishes. What is the symbol for the Aquarian Age?

A. The Fixed Air Sign Aquarius has for its symbol Ganymede, the Cup-Bearer of Zeus. (Originally, the constellation Aquarius was identified with the herm-

aphrodite Egyptian god or *neter* Hapi, who presides over
the source of the Nile and whose being is shrouded in a
certain mystery in consequence of the peculiar sacredness
always ascribed to him.) Ganymede is usually depicted as
a nude young man in a Trojan cap with a mantle thrown
back over his shoulder. He was the most beautiful of all
mortal youths. Zeus was smitten by Ganymede's extra-
ordinary beauty and desired him as his bed-fellow and
favourite. Zeus disguised himself in the form of an eagle
and abducted Ganymede, carrying him off to Mount
Olympus.

Ganymede's father, King Tros of Phrygia, was possessed
by incurable grief at the disappearance of his son and
lamented continually day after day. Zeus finally took pity
on him and gave Tros the magnificent steeds, 'swift as the
storm', that bore the gods, a golden grape vine (the work
of Hephaestus), as well as the promise of immortality for
his son, setting Ganymede's image among the stars as the
constellation Aquarius. When Ganymede's father heard
this message from Zeus, he rejoiced in his heart and
lamented no more.

Ganymede then replaced Hera's daughter, Hebe, as
Zeus' cup-bearer. He brings joy to the eyes of all the gods
by his great beauty. Ganymede functions on Olympus as
Zeus' lover and the server of the red nectar and ambrosia
from the golden mixing bowl to Zeus and the other gods.
His symbol is the cock, a love gift from Zeus.

The word *Ganymede* comes from the two Greek words
ganuesthai and *medea,* which translate, 'rejoicing in
virility'.

Ganymede is comparable to the Vedic Soma who, like
the Trojan youth, was ravished by Indra and changed
into a sparrow-hawk.

88.   Q. What Sign is ruled by the newly discovered planet
      Chiron?

      A. I regard Chiron as a planetoid with much the same
      influences as the asteroids and without zodiacal Sign
      rulership.

89.   Q. Why do you call marriage 'Shadow-Dancing', and
      would you talk more about this?

A. Shadow-Dancing has to do with the physics of partnership and what happens in a partnership situation. The unconscious interaction between the two people involved produces psychic and physical movements which to me seem like dancing – each having to respond or react quickly to the projection coming from the other when they are in the same physical space, each taking as perfectly as possible the unconscious role needs of the other.

Shadow-Dancing occurs at its most unconscious when you marry or legalize a living together relationship with marriage, but it also takes place between roommates and business partners. At the moment of marriage, a contractual partnership, it really seems like the other is separate from you – that you have very little or nothing to do with his or her behaviour as you observe and experience it.

Let me say a little about marriage. We seem to have lost consciousness of what marriage is or could be all about, what it's for and how to best use that particular institution. From my point of view, marriage should be an agreement between two people, regardless of gender, to come together, to remain together willingly, to help each other achieve consciousness and to remain sexually faithful to one another. We understand so little about sexuality and what sexual energy does or can do. We don't realize that marriage forms a container, a pressure cooker if you like, around the two people involved. Sex outside of this partnership vessel literally makes leaks in the transformation vessel called marriage. If you've got leaks, neither of the partners is going to be able to change, to transform. That's what marriage is supposed to be about, where two people come together and agree to help each other through the rebirth process – where both achieve spiritual transformation. Until this process is completed, both must take the responsibility of understanding that what partner 'A' is doing is what partner 'B's' unconscious energies are making him or her do and vice versa.

Marriage is the unconscious agreement on the part of two individuals to accept each other's Shadow projection and live it out. Now the Shadow is the *alter ego* or *other half* of each of us, and it comes into being between birth and seven years of age as we develop an ego, as we go through the sorting process of 'This is me. This isn't me', so that by the age of seven we have formed an ego which we can recognize in the mirror. To maintain this ego and prevent it from dissolving back into the All, an entity of the same sex as ourselves develops on the inner planes. It contains everything we have separated from, positive or negative, good or bad. This is our Shadow. A man has a male Shadow, a woman, a female. This Shadow side of us is projected onto anyone we marry or partner with and communicates to us through them.

The only way I have found to demonstrate this is through astrology. In this way it can be shown that a person's partner is living out the person's Shadow side, because you can read what a person's partner is doing in his or her life and how he or she is behaving all from the person's own horoscope, without looking at or having knowledge of the partner's horoscope.

Until you get to know and come to terms with this Shadow side of yourself, this other half of you (literally the other half of the whole of you), there is no way to really see or understand your partner. When your Shadow is unconscious to you, you're just interacting with that part of yourself that your partner is mirroring for you – and you for your partner, because projection of the Shadows is always a two-way street.

Each of you lives out for the other what the partner doesn't know or accept about himself or herself, positive or negative. Your Shadow projectee may well be living out your best qualities. You may keep thinking, 'I'm the unconscious one with all the hang-ups, and I have this marvellous conscious being for a partner'.

That's your own best stuff you're seeing in your partner, that your partner is showing you. Why not plug it into your own life by becoming conscious of and caring for the Shadow being within you – learning what it needs from you and from your life so that it gets some conscious expression and so it can work with you as friend and conscious partner from within? This would let the Shadow-Dancing relationship, your outer partnership, become that much more joyous and rewarding for both you and your outer partner.

The only way I know to get one's Shadow into consciousness is to meet and work with the Shadow figure in meditation. It is helpful to intellectually understand just what the Shadow is and how it operates. We must first know what it is we're projecting onto our partners despite the unconsciousness of the process. Your Inner Guide will bring your shadow figure to you if you ask him to, and you can get to know that other half of yourself that projects into and manipulates your partner.

Pragmatically in marriage the place to begin is by accepting that your partner is doing exactly what your energies, unconscious though they may be, are manipulating the partner into doing or saying. And you have to take the *full* responsibility of this without saying, 'Well, hey, come on. They're doing something too'. What they're doing in *their* movie, their reality experience, doesn't make any difference. It's what they're doing in *your* movie that carries the message from your Shadow. You have to begin by taking 100% responsibility for that – not 50% or half and half – or the insight will never come. Only when you do take full responsibility (not blame) for your partner's behaviour, for your partner's speech and actions, only then are you in the place of power where you can begin to experience the manipulation of your partner by your Shadow side and begin to bring this energy back to live comfortably in your own life. Then it doesn't have to manipulate your partner into getting its messages to you or doing whatever it is that may be causing the problems between you, causing the barriers or the feelings of separation.

If you truly achieve this and can truly help each other through the transformation process which is set into motion by the coming to terms with and giving personal expression to each of your Shadow sides, then you've completed what the Shadow-Dancing relationship called marriage is really about. Then you should be free to choose to stay together or go your own ways as best of friends. If *both* partners do not achieve this transformation, then I believe they should stay together (till death do them part if necessary), because *both* are unconsciously dragging their feet despite the fact that one will look like the 'good guy'.

Even if you're not married, you have people who live out your Shadow role, people who take your Shadow projection and live it out for you. If you are living with someone on a shared responsibility basis, a roommate or a housemate, they will show you what your Shadow side is like. Anyone you've fathered a child with or conceived a child by (regardless of whether the child was born, stillborn, miscarried or aborted) lives out your Shadow side. The child of your second pregnancy or the second child you've fathered shows you your Shadow, and your Shadow energy onto him or her. But if you've ever gone on want to know how someone's marriage is doing, just look at how their second child is doing. That's how the marriage is doing. That's the child that usually receives both parents' Shadow projections. It's the hardest slot to get born into in a family, because both parents are projecting onto that child – and onto each other – what they're not accepting in themselves.) Your third sibling (brother or sister) – technically, the child of your mother's third pregnancy not counting you – also functions as a Shadow barometer for you, as well as the partner of your marriage partner's or roommate's third brother or sister. Any business partner also lives out your Shadow side as long as the partnership contract is in effect, and all strangers (people we haven't 'role slotted') also take our Shadow projection.

If you've ever tried to change a partner, you already know the impossibility of doing this. Your partner can't change as long as you continue projecting a consistent Shadow energy onto him or her. But if you've ever gone o a real 'I'm going to get my own act together and change' programme and have accomplished this change in yourself you find that your partner automatically changes too. In fact, your partner or Shadow barometer can be on the East Coast and you can be on the West Coast and your partner will still change coincident to your change and new consciousness. Projection has no spatial limitations. You can be in the same house or one of you can be in Russia. In either instance the projection ability remains the same. So the only way to make a change in the Shadow projectee or projectees is to make a change in yourself.

Also, divorce doesn't work so far as the Shadow projection is concerned. No matter how many ex-partners you may have, each of them lives out your Shadow side – you are Shadow-Dancing with each and every one of them, even if you, the ego, don't know where they are on the planet. And when you have a current partner and one or more ex-partners, it usually works out that the current partner lives out the positive aspects of your Shadow side and the ex-partner or partners, the negative aspects.

Try to remember that your partner or anyone who lives out your Shadow side shows you your own hidden qualities, those elements which are unconscious in you. If you take the responsibility for this, treat it as message from the other half of you and act on it, soon you will find Shadow-Dancing to be a dance of joy, not of misery and aggravation.

90.   Q. You say that 'God doesn't take sides'. Then how do we act and make responsible choices in the world if *not* taking sides becomes the model?

A. By examining and meditating on the two aspects of any polarity you must choose between, and then choosing that aspect which best serves your spiritual evolution at that particular time.

91.   Q. How can I become a pure vehicle for the God-force?

A. Perhaps by remembering that purity is not a matter of morality, but a matter of vibration.

92.   Q. The background and landscape where I usually meet the Inner Guide has suddenly changed. Is this a common experience?

A. Changes such as you mention are not uncommon. They generally go along with a new aspect in the relationship with the Guide. Often the landscape evolves and changes along with the individual. All changes in the structural aspects of the meditation are meaningful. Your Guide would be the one who could best explain the significance of the change.

93. Q. I seem to be stuck in my spiritual growth, and, whenever I work on this with my Inner Guide, he takes me to *Death*, who talks about making payments on a loan I took out. What does this have to do with spirituality?

A. *Death*, the Scorpio energy, has to do with both transformation and our indebtedness. One sure way to paralyse one's spiritual transformation is not to pay one's debts. Even a small regular payment on a very large debt keeps the Scorpio area flowing. This is probably what *Death* is trying to say.

94. Q. Are what you call the Aliens and what you call the Adepts the same?

A. I don't think so. The Adepts have expertise in specific reality areas as do the Aliens, but they don't always experience the alienation and rejection common to the Aliens.

95. Q. When you use the word 'Alien' to describe a person, do you mean that the person is from another planet?

A. No. I mean it is *as if* the person were. The so-called Alien individuals perceive and are perceived by outer reality much as if they were non-humans from Mars or Arcturus. They often make others 'nervous', until they accept and assimilate their Alien abilities into consciousness.

96. Q. I never have enough time to accomplish what I want to do in my life, including meditation. What can I do about this?

A. Time, as it is perceived in our outer worlds, has to do with the archetypal energy forms of *The World* and *Old Pan*, Saturn and Capricorn. If one or both of these energy factors is pronounced in your particular horoscope pattern, coming to terms with Time is one of your lessons this life. The secret of expanding Time seems to be to schedule it, from when you wake up in the morning to when you go to bed at night. When Time is structured, it expands. When Time is not structured, it shrinks. Remember to include free time and *play* time in your schedule, otherwise Capricorn and Saturn tend to forget about this use of Time. Don't let your schedule become a straitjacket. Try it out for a while. Then evaluate whether or not it is useful for you and your evolution. If you find it isn't useful or is stultifying in any way, chuck it and make a new schedule for yourself. When you achieve the schedule that *works for you, not you for it,* you will solve your problem with Time.

97.   Q. What do you mean by 'separation'?

A. Inner Guide Meditators seem to use this word a lot: e.g. 'I caught myself separating ten times today' or 'We're separating again'. I use the word to remind myself that what each of us perceives is another aspect of himself, not something separate. The *illusion* of separation, of separateness, is provided by the *Old Pan* archetype. It is his job to maintain this illusion until we are psychologically and spiritually prepared to begin the penetration of the illusion. This learning not to separate takes constant, conscious **PRACTICE**. It is a new way of thinking and feeling about the world, by experiencing the *unity* instead of the separation.

98.   Q. Why is it important for me to ask the archetypes what they need if you say that they will express themselves anyway?

A. If you don't know the needs of your archetypal energies and they remain in the darkness, what they take for their expression may well be what you, the ego, will least like to give. The expressions of an archetype you are working with in meditation and one that is pushed into deep unconsciousness and ignored are quite different, the ego generally labelling the former 'good' or 'positive' and the latter 'bad' or 'negative'.

99.   Q. I am severely affected by 'bummer' movies and TV programmes that I chance to see, and the emotion holds on in me for days. How can I work with this?

A. In your meditation treat the movie or TV programme in exactly the same way you would treat one of your dreams. Heal or transform that which needs it. Question the characters as to what aspects of yourself they are

showing you. *The outer world is literally* all message – from
you, to you. Question your Guide. Some of my most
potent, transformative meditations have been based on
such 'bummer' films.

100. Q. When I gave up some of my bad habits, my partner
seemed to take them over. Why did this happen, and
what can I do about it?

A. This occurs when you, the ego, instead of transforming
the energies that have to do with the habits, suppress or
push against them. The desires are still there – only now
they are unconscious to you. And in a 'Shadow-dancing'
relationship these energies immediately are projected
onto the partner for him or her to live out until you truly
change them in yourself. The need in the ego-Shadow
balance is to raise the middle, that point of balance and
equilibrium between you and your inner Shadow. This
allows consciousness to increase for both you and your
Shadow projectee.

101. Q. Can you suggest other uses for the dream-meditation
journal that you recommend keeping?

A. Jean Bayliss of West Chicago, Illinois, suggests a
monthly *written* evaluation of growth on all levels. Let
your Inner Guide and your Shadow man or woman help
you with this evaluation on the inner planes.

102. Q. I sometimes get a headache after I meditate. What can
I do about this?

A. There seem to be two kinds of headaches people get
from meditating. The first results from forgetting to ask
the Guide whether all has been left in balance in the inner
world or by returning to the body too fast (suddenly
opening your eyes instead of allowing time to get all your
'bodies' back together in one place). This type of headache
is generally frontal. The second type of headache seems
to have to do with what the ego judges to be an overload
of new information from the inner worlds. It makes the
head feel overexpanded. Discussion with your Inner
Guide about either type of headache is the recommend-
ation.

103. Q. Do you use the Inner Guide to go back into lives before this one?

A. Yes, when a continuing problem in this life has its origin in an earlier one. Often it is difficult to work with, say, a fear that seems to have its origin in this life. The experience has impressed itself on the body, and cellular memory won't let go of it. If you learn from the Guide that the fear's origin is in an earlier life, you can go back into that life and transform the fear energy into something more conscious and useful, and this is generally quite easily done. This is because you now have no cellular memory from that life (that body has died), so the resistance isn't there. Stephen Connors of D.O.M.E. Center has developed techniques for working with the Inner Guides on past lives. A change made in a past life changes all your lives. 'Tombstones appear, tombstones disappear', to quote my Guide's comment upon returning from healing and changing one of my past lives. All lives are happening simultaneously.

104. Q. I understand you were once diagnosed as clinically dead and then you came back to life. What was death like?

A. In April, 1953, I experienced my own accidental physical death for seven minutes. This occurred under clinical conditions (my heart was being monitored on an EKG) at the Army Medical Research Laboratory in Fort Knox, Kentucky. The entire experience happened in full consciousness. There was no break in my awareness between the time my heart stopped beating and when it spontaneously started again seven minutes later. For a sceptic like me, it was one of the most important experiences of my life. Among the things I learned was: 'If it isn't beautiful, you're not dead' and also what true freedom is. This certain knowledge removed forever my fears of death and replaced them with understanding.

105. Q. If your heart stopped for seven minutes, why didn't you get brain damage?

A. The experience took place at 40° below zero. I was refrigerated.

106. Q. Is what is called the 'double' the same as the Shadow?

A. I believe so. In Europe there is a folk belief about the double or *Doppelgänger:* You see your double and you die. This seems to be psychologically true. As you work in the Inner Guide Meditation with your Shadow man or woman, the figure will come to look more and more like you. The day the figure looks *exactly* like you, as if you were looking into a mirror, is the day you will experience an ego death and rebirth. When the death-rebirth process is completed, your Shadow will again look unlike you. You can always tell where you are in your own transformation process by looking at your shadow.

107. Q. For years now it has seemed that time has speeded up. What accounts for this?

A. The planet Pluto is the generation marker and has to do with the illusion of things changing around us. Pluto usually takes 30 years to go through a Sign of the zodiac, but since the mid-Sixties Pluto has been speeding up and now it is about to go through a Sign in 11 years. It doesn't slow down again and go back to 30 year generations until the late Nineties. In a sense we're moving toward getting almost three-days in one, and things appear to be changing more rapidly around us.

108. Q. What do you mean by 'You get what you attend to?'

A. Energy follows attention. There is at every moment a 100% positive and a 100% negative universe available to each of us. Our energy goes to where our attention is focused and feeds that. If we, say, go through the evening newspaper and read all the 'bummer' news, we are in effect increasing the probability of 'bummers' in our lives. If we can learn to focus on the 'pluses' in our realities, those thereby are fed and increase in our individual realities.

109. Q. I have trouble meditating when it is daylight or the room is bright. What can I do about this?

A. People with prominent Neptune, Pisces or Twelfth House factors in their charts (Sun, Moon or Ascendant in conjunction with Neptune; Sun, Moon or Ascendant in Pisces; or with the Sun or Moon in the Twelfth House) are extremely light-sensitive. A sleeping mask, called a 'hoodwink', will generally take care of this problem.

110. Q. I find that many things irritate me. How can I deal with this?

A. Irritants show us where we are being vague about our rules or structures. If possible, learn to say 'No' to the things that irritate you, or to compromise if the irritant has to do with another. In either case, use the irritants as messages about what you do allow and what you don't allow in your life and just where you are being vague about these areas.

111. Q. I have an aversion to both flies and spiders. What do they represent in my unconscious?

A. Flies are related to the *Old Pan* or *Devil* archetype, and spiders, to *The High Priestess*. You will generally attract flies when one of your 'Shoulds' or 'Shouldn'ts' is activated, and spiders when your security system is being rattled. Ask *Old Pan* or *The High Priestess* why their messengers were sent and what the message is that you're not hearing or listening to.

112. Q. When I am extremely ego involved in something and can't get a clear answer from the Guide or the archetypes, how can I resolve this?

A. You might try asking the Inner Guide, before you go to sleep, to send a dream that will answer your question. When you receive the dream, the Guide can then help you decipher it. In this way material from your unconscious can get past your ego defences.

113. Q. You speak of certain archetypes as being associated with specific parts of the body. Is the Inner Guide associated with any part of the body?

A. Yes. The Guide is associated with the solar plexus, the Jupiter *chakra* or energy centre in the body. Our gut feelings are often messages from our Inner Guides.

114. Q. Do you feel that superstitions and hang-ups of the Piscean Age, such as circumcision, will carry over into the Aquarian Age?

A. In general, no. Circumcision, however, is more a problem of our cultural materialism and ignorance, than of superstition or hang-up. Marc Edmund Jones in his book, *Occult Philosophy*, gives the following information: 'Circumcision is the excision of the male prepuce (or the similar operation on the female internal labia, not historically of any but therapeutic significance) which as a religious ceremony dramatizes the necessity of self-preparation for the enjoyment of social values through a conscious redirection of control of physical sensation. It is the preparatory rite for MATRIMONY primarily, and for the ALCHEMICAL MARRIAGE ultimately. The ALCHEMICAL MARRIAGE of the esoteric tradition presents a divine self-unification as the supreme goal of all initiation. This is marked, physiologically, by the development of an actual nerve tract' [as the result of the circumcision] 'composed of white nerve tissue which links the brain areas containing the pineal and pituitary glands, respectively, and facilitates the exalted immediacies of high illumination.'[2] The rite of circumcision comes to us from the ancient Egyptians, and it facilitates the spiritual awakening or Enlightenment experience.

115. Q. If you were to think up an Aquarian Age motto, what would it be?

A. 'How can I help?' would be my nomination for a motto for the Age of Aquarius, because the coming age is an age of cooperation, of individual and group effort. If each of us could keep consciously in mind at all times, *How can I help?*, the transition from the old to the new could take place much more harmoniously. How can I help the person doing what I can't do for the coming times? How can I help, and on what level? – the spiritual? – the mental? – the emotional? – the material? How am I best equipped to help? What do I have that others need? How can I best share what I have?

If we can first establish what it is that we have in order to help and then the direction we would like to see that help move in, the necessary actions will become self-evident. Perhaps I can help by giving material support to a person or a group that I believe is doing something important for the coming times. Perhaps I can help by calling on those in emotional turmoil, lending an ear to those who have no listeners. Perhaps I can help by sending the book or the idea which might be the necessary key or catalyst for someone. Perhaps I can help by sending love consciously to those in need. There are many ways each of us can find to help, to share in the coming adventure.

But when you find how you can help – *ACT ON IT!* Don't procrastinate. NOW is when the help is needed. As the old saw goes, 'The road to hell is paved with good intentions'.

116. Q. If I'm gay, would my Inner Guide ask me to change or give up my sexual orientation in order to be able to unite with my God-Centre?

A. The Inner Guides put no one down for his or her sexual orientation. But the requirements of one's God-Centre are another matter. The ego, that person you see in the mirror and call yourself, must be willing to let go of or take on *any role* or anything else required by its God-Centre. Maybe your Centre will ask that you be celibate or heterosexual. Maybe, if you were now heterosexual, your Centre would ask for homosexual expression or no sexual expression at all. If you were married, you might be asked to put the marriage aside. If you were unmarried, your Centre might ask you to marry.

One never knows what the requirements of one's own God-Centre are going to be. But try not to worry about it. Our Centres generally ask for ego role changes when the ego is prepared for and willing to make them.

But if your will to unite with God, your seeking of Enlightenment or permanent Kundalini arousal and balance is phrased in your mind along the lines of 'I'll do anything my God-Centre asks me to do *except for . . .'* forget it! The one thing you are unwilling to do or don't want to do will block all the rest of your spiritual work until you overcome such resistance to the will of your Centre. On the spiritual path your sexual orientation is totally irrelevant. Love will never separate you from God, no matter what its variety.

117. Q. When I do my daily meditations, I find that the information and experiences I receive from the archetypes are things that have already been in my mind. How can I achieve deeper levels with the Inner Guide Meditation?

A. At D. O. M. E. Center we schedule meditations together daily. We also discovered what you are experiencing was happening in some of us. What we now do is *a series of three meditations on the same subject.*

For instance, if we are meditating on the Love-Creation energy form (often experienced as a Solar figure) and the Moon or Mother archetypes, we will first have our Inner Guides bring these two figures together with us and ask what they need from each other and from us in our daily lives to work in harmony as energies within us. It is during this initial meditation that those thoughts that have already been in our minds become more specific and those rationalizations provided by our minds in terms of these two archetypal energy forms come into clear form. But generally during this first meditation, nothing new comes forth – nothing that will change the ego in any way in terms of its thoughts, actions or behaviours. We record this initial meditation.

We then go back with our Guides and encounter the same two energy forms once again. Ego resistance is noted during this second encounter, as the mind has already given all it contained in terms of rationalization and logic during the first meditation. But as we remain in the presence of the two figures with our Guides, new information and insights, new symbols present themselves with a life quality not experienced in the first meditation. We then record and discuss this second meditation, and the group experiences the new life quality and freshness in itself among its members.

We then meditate a third time on the same energy forms, and it is during this third meditation that the deep level information and energy comes forth and affects our ego personalities, causing a deeper unity between ourselves and our inner and outer worlds.

118. Q. What is it that you consider you are doing when you are interacting with the archetypal energy forms? For instance, if you are using the tarot images, such as *The Fool* or *The Hanged Man*, just what does your mind judge is going on?

A. I consider myself to be making friends with and assimilating different aspects of myself and of the Oneness.

119. Q. You speak of the necessity of a person having three absolute No's. Why?

A. In a three dimensional reality it seems that three absolute No's are necessary for reality stability. Less than three make reality too wobbly, and more than three make it too rigid. Earlier in this book, I speak of the Law of No, which I would suggest reviewing.

One's No's are most useful if they are not imbued with morality. Try to keep the concepts of Good and Evil, Right and Wrong, Good and Bad out of your thinking mechanism, and replace them with the thoughts, 'This is *useful* for my spiritual evolution,' and, 'This is *not useful* for my spiritual evolution.'

If you have labelled something 'Good' and three or four years go by and it becomes destructive to you, it is difficult to let go of it because of the label of 'Good'. The label makes whatever is labelled Good 'sticky' and hard to let go of. But if you had labelled the same thing 'useful to my spiritual evolution', it would be easy to let it go when you discover it has become no longer of any use to you or to your growth.

The three absolute No's do not necessarily have to have anything to do with moral or ethical issues or considerations. Perhaps the only absolute No's you can discover that you have currently are, 'I will not kill anyone under any circumstances', and 'I will never smoke marijuana'. In terms of usefulness, the No, 'I will never wear the colour orange until I make the conscious decision to change this absolute No to another,' will suffice as the third.

No's are structural. Our absolute No's make the walls, floors and ceiling of our reality boxes, as I have mentioned previously, and the qualified No's – the Maybe's – are the doors and windows. Yes is not structural. It is space, inside and out. When you change a No to a Maybe, a Maybe to a Yes, or invent a new absolute No, you literally change the structure of both your inner and outer realities.

120. A. You speak of a four-body system. What are the four bodies?

A. The most apparent of our four bodies is the physical or earth body. It's our anchor to the material plane. Without it our three inner bodies would have no transformation vehicle, no 'pot to cook in' for the alchemical change. Then there's the mental or air body. Every thought you think or idea you have occurs in that body. Next is the astral or water body – the emotional body. Every feeling you have, every sensation you feel, takes place in that body. It has the same form as the physical and is the body you perceive in an out-of-the-body experience or upon death. The fourth body and the least dense is our spiritual or fire body – the love body. The ability to give love, to create, occurs from that body. It is the body you experience when you feel your life quality, the sense that 'I am'. The three upper bodies interpenetrate each other, and all penetrate the physical body giving us our life and animation.

121. Q. I began working with my Inner Guide, and he introduced me to one of the archetypal figures who said he wouldn't interact with me or give me any information until I got a job and a permanent place to live. Then I met several other of the archetypes who said the same thing. Are these just reflections of my old materialistic hang-ups getting in the way of my spiritual growth through the 'Magic Mirror Effect' or could this be true?

A. To separate the material from the spiritual is false in my opinion. If everything is One, what isn't holy? Spiritual growth can often be compared to a pyramid. The bottom of the pyramid is the physical plane. If this isn't solid, there is no base for spirit. This may be why you are getting the messages about a job and a home from the archetypes. Without this firm earth plane base the changes brought from archetypal interaction would create too much turmoil in your life.

It is common for archetypes initially to request a stabilization of the earth plane. Sometimes it takes the form of dietary requests, sometimes, getting a health problem taken care of, and often, requesting much the same things requested of you. To handle highly intense spiritual energy – the energy of the archetypes – a strong material base is necessary.

122. Q. How can I learn to visualize colour more strongly in my meditations?

A. David Philip Benge of D.O.M.E. has come up with a very useful technique to develop the ability of seeing colour in meditation: 'Get a 75 to 100 watt incandescent light bulb and lamp. Set it up on a stand and look directly at it for 30 to 45 seconds. Then cover your eyes with your palms, being careful not to touch the eyelids themselves. (The bright light will not harm your eyes. In fact this is a method used in the Bates Method of eye exercises.) The optic nerve will pick up the impression of the bare bulb, and you will 'see', with your eyes closed, a series of colours in the same shape and outline as the bulb.

'When I do this exercise, I see orange, followed by meadow green, then magenta, then violet, and finally deep purple. Your brain will remember and record this colour experience, and you will be able to apply these colours to your meditative life. Becoming adept in the Inner Guide Meditation has a lot to do with re-training yourself to bring together mental and emotional aspects within yourself. This colour exercise does much to develop the mental application of colour to your meditations.'

It is also useful to visualize the inner colours as iridescent. Iridescence seems to be strongly connected with spirit. Practice by looking at sea shells, iridescent butterfly wings, iridescent insects and the iridescence found in the feathers of birds. Seeing the inner colours as iridescent brings much power into the meditative experience.

123. Q. How can I work with my Inner Guide to allow energy to flow more easily in my physical body? I have a lot of problems with stiffness and aches and pains in certain parts of my body.

A. In the meditation call on *The Sun,* and ask *The Sun* to radiate those specific areas of your body corresponding to the horoscopic House Saturn is in, the Sign Saturn is in and the House of the horoscope that has Capricorn on its Cusp. For instance, if you have Saturn in Sagittarius in the 5th House, you would ask *The Sun* to radiate and create energy flow in the liver, buttocks, hips and thighs (Sagittarius), the heart (5th House) and the stomach (4th House, the House with Capricorn on the Cusp). Our bodies tend to block energy in these specific areas, and giving them this conscious attention removes not only physical problems, but also out-in-the-world problems the Saturn-Capricorn energies may be causing.

If you have further questions relating to any aspect of the Inner Guide Meditation, or, if you would like to share some of your own meditation experiences or insights, please send them to: D.O.M.E., the Inner Guide Meditation Center, P.O. Box 25358, Colorado Springs, Colorado 80936, U.S.A. We'll try to answer the questions in forthcoming books or articles and to publish the shared information in *Aquarian Changes*, D.O.M.E.'s quarterly journal. (We'll send you a sample copy on request.)

[1] Carl G. Jung, *Psychological Types,* ed H. Read, M. Fordham, G. Adler, W. McGuire, trans. R.F.C. Hull, *The Collected Works of C. G. Jung,* Bollingen Series XX, Vol. 6 (Princeton University Press, 1971), p.428.

[2] Marc Edmund Jones, *Occult Philosophy* (Stanwood, Wash. Sabian Publ. Soc., 1971), p.298, 333.

'Tree of Life' Sphere *Binah* from the D.O.M.E. Meditation Cards by Sheila W. Ross.

THE
INNER GUIDE MEDITATION

Part IV

Trump of *The Hermit* from the Rider-Waite Tarot Deck.

Trump of *The Moon* from the Rider-Waite Tarot Deck.

11.

How to Translate a Horoscope into Tarot Terms for a Worksheet

The 'Horoscope-Tarot Equivalents' pages which follow this section list the tarot equivalents for the eight planets, Sun, Moon and the twelve Signs of the zodiac. (For instance, Aries= *The Emperor,* mercury = *the Magician,* etc.) Utilizing these tarot equivalents, the Worksheet is designed to give the astrological relationships, in image form, between the energies in the individual's natal horoscope, so that the inner planes may be approached in a structured way. (In calculating aspects in the original horoscopes, an orb of influence of 15°, plus or minus, is allowed for solar aspects, 12° for lunar aspects and 8° for planetary aspects, if the aspect is a conjunction, square, opposition or trine: 6° for solar and lunar aspects and 5° for planetary aspects, If the aspect is a quincunx of sextile; and 3° for a quintile. Parallels of declination are allowed an orb of 1° for the planets and 1½° for the Sun and Moon.) The Worksheet is divided into sections, each representing a particular way of approaching or relating to the energies involved in a personal horoscope pattern.

I. High Energy Relationships

These pairs of Tarot archetypes represent the *squares* (90° relationships or aspects), the *oppositions* (180° relationships) and *the opposing zodiacal fields*: Aries and Libra, Taurus and Scorpio, Gemini and Sagittarius, Cancer and Capricorn, Leo and Aquarius, and Virgo and Pisces.

All these pairs represent those energies that the individual was born with in an unconscious non-cooperation, polarization or conflict relationship. They function to create the pain and problems of the life. After coming to terms individually with each member of a particular pair, ask your Inner Guide to bring the two archetypes together with you and the Guide. Explain to the archetypes that when they fight, act separately or refuse to cooperate as energies within you, it causes pain, injury and destruction in *your* life and around you. Ask them what they need from each other to begin working together in harmony as energies within you. First ask one what it needs from the other to be willing and able to work with it in harmony and cooperation. Then ask the same of the second. If an impasse occurs, remind them again that they hurt *you* by this behaviour. When they become conscious and cooperating, this constructive energy flows into one's life. Therefore, the squares and oppositions are, in potential, the 'best' aspects of one's horoscope, because they have the most strength.

After the two archetypal energy forms have communicated what they need from each other to begin cooperating within you, ask them to join hands with each other and with you and the Guide. When you have made this circle of hands and you can *feel* the grip of each entity holding your hand and can feel the texture and other qualities of the skin of the hands you hold, give the two archetypes permission to balance their energies *with* each other and *in* you. At this point you will feel strange sensations in your body as the energies shift and rebalance within you. Note which specific body areas you feel being affected. Allow the energies to flow until the Guide breaks the circle. Then ask them what you can do in your everyday life to help them stay in harmony within you.

II. Unions

The 'Check Union Between' section of the Worksheet includes the *conjunctions* (0° relationships), *parallels* (0° relationships of declination), *sextiles* (60° relationships), *quincunxes* (150° relationships), and *quintiles* (72° relationships) of a natal horoscope. These Unions represent energies in the pattern that, according to theory, *should* be working together. They seldom are in conflict, but often they are acting separately. When in the presence of the two with the Inner Guide, ask what they need from each other and from your life (in terms of action, thought or behaviour) to aid in their harmonious union.

III. Basic Archetypes

The 'Basic Archetypes' are the *final dispositors* of the horoscope, with the Sun and its Sign and the Ruler of the Ascendant and its Sign added if they are not included in the group of final dispositors. These represent the 'last vote' forces within the individual. No matter what the current ego may desire, these are the energies that receive the final say over every area of the individual reality. Treat the 'Basic Archetype' group, your Shadow and your Inner Guide as your *board of advisors* or *board of directors*. The final dispositors always include planets in their Rulership, e.g., Saturn in Capricorn, planets in 'mutual reception', each planet in the Sign ruled by the other, e.g., Moon in Scorpio and Pluto in Cancer, and all 'planetary chains'. (For further information on final dispositors, see Thyrza Escobar's fine book, *Essentials of Natal Interpretation.*)

IV. The Circles of Hands

The section labelled 'Circle of Hands with' identifies specific *energy groups* of the individual natal chart and always includes the Cardinal, Fixed and Mutable *Grand Cross* grouping: e.g. the Cardinal signs: Aries, Cancer, Libra and Capricorn; the Fixed signs: Taurus, Leo, Scorpio and Aquarius; and the Mutable signs: Gemini, Virgo, Sagittarius and Pisces. Also included in this section are the planetary groupings formed by the classical astrological patterns of the *T-Cross*, the *Grand Trine*, the *Grand Square* and the *Yod Cross* or *Finger of God* configuration.

In addition to these, individual groupings consisting of three or more planets forming high energy relationships that connect to one another in the natal chart are included for a 'Circle of Hands'. For instance, if the planet Saturn were squaring a conjunction of the Sun and Mars in a natal pattern, included in this section would be a circle of hands with the Tarot *World, Sun* and *Tower*.

The Shadow man or woman, the 'High Energy Relationship' pairs, the 'Unions' and the figures making up the 'Basic Archetypes' also are included in the 'Circle of Hands' section.

It is recommended that these circles of hands be done on a periodic basis. The planetary, zodiacal and combination forms are *living* energies each of us carries within. As we go through the various cycles and rhythms of our lives, some of the energies may go out of balance with the others. For instance, in a Mutable Sign grouping of *The Lovers, The Hermit, Temperance* and *The Moon*, whenever you meditate with them and ask them to do a circle of hands, *The Hermit* may be out of balance and not cooperating or antagonistic to the others in the group. What to do in such an instance is to ask the entire group what *you* can do new or stop doing in terms of action, thought or behaviour in your daily outer life to allow them all to remain in balance and cooperating with each other within you. And ask also what you may be doing in your life to keep *The Hermit*, in this instance, out of balance with the rest of the energies.

End each interaction, whether with a pair, your Shadow or with a larger group, by asking the participants to take hands with each other and with you *and your Guide* forming a circle of hands. It is important to really *be there* in your body looking out of your eyes and not watching yourself in the scene. Feel the textures of the hands you hold, the Guide on your right (if right handed) and the archetypes or energy combinations to your left. Give them permission to balance their energies *with* each other and *in* you. You will *feel* the energy shift and change within your body as the archetypal energies balance themselves in your system. Each pair or group will cause sensations in specific areas of your body, and each circle grouping will feel different than the others. Feel the sensations and note their locations in your body. If the sensation or feeling flow is weak, ask for increased intensity, always making sure that you are *in* your body and in full possession of *all* your senses. If you are not *in* your inner world or astral body, you are disconnected and will feel nothing. Let your Guide be the one to break the circle.

V. The Alien Energy Constructs

The Alien patterns are specific planetary placements, unions and absences of planets and the Ascendant in certain zodiacal Signs which produce highly specialized individuals.

The Alien *Powers* are those with the Sun in conjunction with Saturn, Uranus, Neptune or Pluto (allowing a 15° orb). They have the ability to *extend* or *radiate* their specialized energy field out into the physical plane, affecting and changing whatever it touches. It is a *high priest* function, in the ancient sense, whether in a male or female body.

The Alien *Vessels* are individuals born with the Moon in

conjunction with Saturn, Uranus, Neptune or Pluto (allowing a 12° orb). Their action is *magnetic,* drawing specialized energies out of those around them. They also function as 'doors' to other spaces. Theirs is a *high priestess* function, in the ancient sense, whether their physical vehicles are female or male.

The Alien *Instruments* are people who have Saturn, Uranus, Neptune or Pluto in the *First House* of their natal horoscope or *conjunct the Ascendant* (Cusp of the First House) *from the Twelfth House* (allowing an orb of 8°). They function as *amplifiers* of one of the four primary planetary energies in those around them. Their abilities are intrinsic to their physical bodies. Nerve pathways and even bodily organs often are in atypical anatomical positions, enabling them, without injury, to act as specialized energy receivers and broadcasters.

Some Alien patterns may be the result of 'mutual reception', two planets each in the Rulership Sign of the other, e.g., Sun in Cancer, Moon in Leo. The planets literally become interchangeable. (This Alien factor was discovered by Norma Gremore of Cedar Crest, New Mexico.)

All the before mentioned Aliens have the ability to contain and to radiate energies which in a non-Alien being would blow the circuits unless the body and psyche had been trained and prepared to receive and radiate them. Even the Aliens have trouble with their abilities, which often frighten and disturb them – especially when these abilities awaken unexpectedly. (It is interesting to note that individuals with non-Alien patterns, who are drawn to work and be with Aliens, develop paranormal abilities much more rapidly than the Aliens. This may be because they have not developed the early suppression and defence mechanisms that the Aliens have.)

Another group of Aliens, termed the *Adepts,* are individuals born with neither the Ascendant nor planets in a particular *Quality* (Cardinal, Fixed or Mutable Signs) or *Element* (Fire, Earth, Air or Water Signs). These individuals have an *expertise,* not a lack, in the particular Quality or Element missing in their birth pattern. These Aliens are:

The Cardinal Adepts – Cardinal Quality absent.
The Fixed Adepts – Fixed Quality absent.
The Mutable Adepts – Mutable Quality absent.
The Fire Adepts – Fire Element absent.
The Earth Adepts — Earth Element absent.

The Air Adepts – Air Element absent.

The Water Adepts – Water Element absent.

Children and adults who remain virgin seem to be *un-programmed* and are like gelatin which has never set. That is to say, they seem to easily be able to develop the abilities of any of the Aliens, so long as the condition of virginity is maintained Heterosexual intercourse in which the male has no orgasm during penetration does not appear to interfere with the state of virginity or the availability of the powers of Alien abilities in the man, unless the woman has orgasm while penetration occurs. If neither the man nor the woman have orgasm while penetration occurs, the woman's virginity is maintained. Masturbation and homosexual expression also do not seem to interfere with the virgin state. This is probably the reason that celibacy and/or a virgin condition were, and often still are, pre-requisite in many religions and spiritual practices in the world.

It is to be remembered that the Alien abilities function in the individual possessing them whether he or she is conscious of them or not, and they cause the life symptom patterns mentioned earlier in the book.

To work with an Alien energy form, ask *all* the archetypes that make up one *Alien Energy Construct* to line up in a row, then ask them to dissolve into their raw energy components and to re-form as a single human or humanoid figure. Then ask the Alien to set up his or her kind of classroom and to begin teaching you the mysteries, powers and abilities you were born with that the Alien represents, supervised by your Inner Guide.

It seems useful to ask the *Powers* to take male forms, the *Vessels* to take female forms, and the *Instruments* to take the sex of the person possessing the construct. Let the *Adepts* take whichever sex they choose.

VI. Consciousness Resistant Factors

Certain astrological factors in a natal horoscope produce internal energies which resist assimilation by the ego, creating problems from the unconscious in the individual's life in the life areas ruled by or corresponding to these energies. These factors are planets in their *Rulership* or *Exaltation* Signs in women and planets in the *Fall* or *Detriment* Signs in men, as well as the Signs on the Cusps of the Seventh and Twelfth Houses (if there are no planets in those Signs in the Sixth or Eleventh Houses), Intercepted Signs with no planets in them, and all planets *in* the Seventh and Twelfth Houses. The following lists of planets in these Signs are:

Consciousness Resistant Factors in Men
Sun in Aquarius – *Sun* and *Star*
Sun in Libra – *Sun* and *Justice*
Moon in Capricorn – *High Priestess* and *Old Pan*
Moon in Scorpio – *High Priestess* and *Death*
Mercury in Sagittarius – *Magician* and *Temperance*
Mercury in Pisces – *Magician* and *Moon*
Mercury in Leo – *Magician* and *Strength*
Venus in Scorpio – *Empress* and *Death*
Venus in Aries – *Empress* and *Emperor*
Venus in Virgo – *Empress* and *Hermit*
Mars in Libra – *Tower* and *Justice*
Mars in Cancer – *Tower* and *Chariot*
Jupiter in Gemini – *Wheel of Fortune* and *Lovers*
Jupiter in Capricorn – *Wheel of Fortune* and *Old Pan*
Saturn in Cancer – *World* and *Chariot*
Saturn in Aries – *World* and *Emperor*
Uranus in Leo – *Fool* and *Strength*
Uranus in Taurus – *Fool* and *High Priest*
Neptune in Virgo – *Hanged Man* and *Hermit*
Neptune in Gemini – *Hanged Man* and *Lovers*
Pluto in Taurus – *Last Judgement* and *High Priest*
Pluto in Aquarius – *Last Judgement* and *Star*

Consciousness Resistant Factors in Women
Sun in Aries – *Sun* and *Emperor*
Sun in Leo – *Sun* and *Strength*
Moon in Taurus – *High Priestess* and *High Priest*
Moon in Cancer – *High Priestess* and *Chariot*
Mercury in Aquarius – *Magician* and *Star*
Mercury in Gemini – *Magician* and *Lovers*
Mercury in Virgo – *Magician* and *Hermit*
Venus in Pisces – *Empress* and *Moon*
Venus in Taurus – *Empress* and *High Priest*
Venus in Libra – *Empress* and *Justice*
Mars in Capricorn – *Tower* and *Old Pan*

Mars in Aries – *Tower* and *Emperor*
Jupiter in Cancer – *Wheel of Fortune* and *Chariot*
Jupiter in Sagittarius – *Wheel of Fortune* and *Temperance*
Saturn in Libra – *World* and *Justice*
Saturn in Capricorn – *World* and *Old Pan*
Uranus in Scorpio – *Fool* and *Death*
Uranus in Aquarius – *Fool* and *Star*
Neptune in Sagittarius – *Hanged Man* and *Temperance*
Neptune in Pisces – *Hanged Man* and *Moon*
Pluto in Leo – *Last Judgement* and *Strength*
Pluto in Scorpio – *Last Judgement* and *Death*

The two energies which have to do with the planet and the Sign may be asked to combine into a *third* figure which represents *both* energies. For instance, if the Moon is in the Sign Cancer, ask the two tarot forms, *High Priestess* and *Chariot*, to merge into a third form which contains the combined energy of both. Ask your Inner Guide to supervise this process.

VII. The Special Constructs

A circular diagram is drawn for each of the classical astrological patterns: the *T-Cross* (as in the example horoscope on page 179), *the Grand Trine,* the *Grand Square* and the *Yod Cross.* These are drawn to indicate how to position the archetypes for a 'circle of hands'. The circle is viewed from above. In the example the Inner Guide is at the Ninth House point, I, 'Edwin', am to his left, and the other archetypal forms are positioned around in a circle to my left. *The World*, in the example, would then be holding the Guide's right hand completing the circle.

These special constructs are titled: *T-Cross Energy Balancing Construct, Grand Square Energy Balancing Construct, Grand Trine Activation Construct* and *Yod Cross Construct.*

VIII. No Alien Patterns in the Horoscope

Horoscopes without Alien constructs have the possibilities of the full range of human potential without the specialization of the Aliens. They don't seem to have the resistances in meditation which the Aliens have to push through. (Examples of people without Alien constructs in their natal horoscopes will be found later in the book.)

12.

Horoscope-Tarot Equivalents

The names given in parentheses are other titles for the Major Trumps or Arcana of the tarot cards and are given for further suggestion.

0   **Uranus** – *Fool* (Adam-Kadmon, The Babe in the Egg on the Lotus, the Vagabond, Breath, Lightning, The April Fool, The Invisible Point Which Is Not, The Green Giant of Spring, The Jester, Unity of Centre-Circumference, The Knight-Errant, The Unconscious Self, The Stranger in a Strange Land, The Wanderer, Aboriginal Chaos, Tao, Spirit, The Joker, The Great Void, The Babe in the Abyss, Dionysius, Krishna, Divine Folly, Harparkrat, The Divine Bum, Freedom, The Holy Ghost, The Eccentric, Spirit of Aether, Fiery Intelligence, The Crown of Wisdom).

1   **Mercury** – *Magician* (The Magus, The Juggler, The Magus of Power, The Initiate, Tahuti, The Pagat, The Mountebank, Hermes, St. Christopher, Loki, Harlequin, The Trickster, Thoth, The Messenger of the Gods, The Minstrel, The Being, Christ, The Wizard, The Conjurer, Prometheus, Logic, The Occultist, Creative Will, Intelligence of Transparency, The Crown of Understanding).

2   **The Moon** – *High Priestess* (Initiation, The Divine Sophia, The Binary, The Female Pontiff, The Archpriestess, Hecate, Pope Joan, The Priestess of the Silver Star, The Wise Woman, The Witch, The Yoni, Door of the Hidden Sanctuary, The Vesica Piscis, Gnosis, Veiled Isis, The Virgin Mother of the World, Moira, The Holy Guardian, Hathor, Juno, Hera Anima, Diana, The Receiver of All, The Vagina, Soul of All Light, Artemis, Goddess of the Night, The

'Tree of Life' engraving from *Geheime Figuren der Rosenkreuzer* (1785).

Pillars, Joachim and Boaz, The Huntress, Trivia, Nuit, Virgin Mary, The Veil of Maya, The Madonna, Uniting Intelligence, Memory, The Good Mother, The Crown of Beauty).

3   **Venus** – *Empress* (Aphrodite, Isis Unveiled, Eve, Lilith, Mother Nature, Isis-Urania, Demeter, The Queen, Daughter of the Mighty Ones, Objective Reality, Alchemical Salt, Gate of the Equilibrium of the Universe, The Eternally Pregnant, Kali, Ma, The Corn Woman, The Magma Mater, Love, The Gate of Heaven, Astarte, The Love of Master and Student in the Mysteries, Wife, Luminous Intelligence, Imagination, The Wisdom of Understanding).

4. **Aries** – *Emperor* (Tetragrammaton, Sun of the Morning, God as Father and Maker, Osiris, Guardian of the Holy Grail, The Cubic Stone, Alchemical Sulphur, The Law of Four, Hermetic Philosophy, Ho Nike, The King, The Ka'ba, The Conqueror, Mars, Ares, Lightning, Chief Among the Mighty Ones, Priapus, The All-Father, Athena, Minerva, Spiritual Illumination, The Beginning, The I Am, He Who Sees and Sets in Order, The First One, The Initiator, First Logos, The Higher Self, Lord, Father of the Sun, Husband, Hercules, Spiritual Governor, The Man of War, The Stone Cube, Constituting Intelligence, Reason, Sight, The Wisdom of Sovereignty and Beauty).

5   **Taurus** – *High Priest* (The Hierophant, Pope, Grand Master, Master of the Secrets, The Gypsy Prince, Hierarch, Archpriest, Magus of the Eternal, The Prince, He Who Hears and Teaches to Hear, Revealer of the Holy, Universal Law, Master, Voice of the True Self, The Listening of the Silence, The Physical Voice of Triumph and Eternal Intelligence, Triumphant and Eternal Intelligence, Intuition, Hearing, The Wisdom and Fountain of Mercy).

6   **Gemini** – *Lovers* (The Parting of the Ways, Eros, Cupid, The Two Ways, The Dual Brain, The Children of the Voice, Oracle of the Mighty Gods, The Judgement of Paris, The Divine Androgyne, Anubis, Andromeda's Rescue, The Student, Thinking Perfected, Hermes, The Connection, Duality, Twinning, The Angel Raphael, The Creation of the World, Old Pan's Servant, Castor and Pollux, Temptation, Choice, The Alchemical or Hermetic Marriage of the Elements, Division, Separation, The Attractions of

Opposites, Disposing Intelligence, The Understanding of
Beauty, The Production of Beauty and Sovereignty).

7 **Cancer** – *Chariot* (The King in Triumph, The Charioteer,
The Chariot of Osiris, Chaos, Home, The Fence, The Box,
The Children of the Powers of the Waters, The Driver, Lord
of the Triumph of Light, The Conqueror, Unification,
Reconciliation, He Who Bears the Holy Grail, Self Control,
Progress, The People, Intelligence of the House of Influence,
Victory, Birth-Death, The Chariot of Reincarnation, The
Ark, Receptivity, Understanding Acting on Severity).

8 **Leo** – *Strength* (Force, Power, Lust, Fortitude, The
Conquered Lion, The Devil's Phallus, Lucifer Trans-
formed, The Muzzled Lion, The Daughter of the Flaming
Sword, Samson, The Enchantress, The Strength of Love,
Union, Ecstasy, The Snake of Knowledge and Delight, The
Lion-Headed Serpent, Vital Power, Prana, Dichotomy
Resolved, Neith, Intelligence of the Secret of All Spiritual
Activities, Intelligence of the Secret of Works, The
Emperor's Love, Mercy Tempering Severity).

9 **Virgo** – *Hermit* (Truth, The Sage, The Old One, Prudence,
Occult Light, The Path to Initiation, Adonis, Attis, The
Secret Seed, The Spermatozoon, The Prophet of the
Eternal, The Pilgrim Soul, The Veiled Lamp, Magus of the
Voice of Power, Perfected Love, The Virgin, Inner Know-
ledge, Light and Force, Intelligence of Will, Capuchin,
Diogenes, The Perfected Tool, The Harpy, Response,
Coition, The Old Man, The Hunchback, The Mercy of
Beauty, The Magnificence of Sovereignty).

10 **Jupiter** – *Wheel of Fortune* (Chance, Fortune, The Law of
Karma, Tarot, The Sphinx, Lord of the Forces of Life, The
Three Fates, The Gambler, The Guru, The Three-Headed
One, Zeus, The Circle of Time, Excess, Rota, Rotation,
Major Fortune, True Will, The Law of the Wheel, Wealth
and Poverty, Intelligence of Conciliation, Rewarding Intel-
ligence of Those Who Seek, Expansion, Lucky, Lady Luck,
The Guide Force, The Mercy and Magnificence of Victory).

11 **Libra** – *Justice* (Adjustment, The Sword and the Balance,
Union of Opposites, Copulation, The Judge, Daughter of
the Lords of Truth, The Jury, Ruler of the Balance, The

Blind One, Karma in Action, The Mirror, Inner Truth, Nephthys, Athena, The Partner, The Shadow, The Scales, The Other, The Stranger, The Crystal Cube, Narcissus, Equilibrium, Transition, Faithful Intelligence, The Severity of Beauty and Sovereignty).

12 **Neptune** – *Hanged Man* (The Sacrifice, Spirit of the Mighty Waters, The Thief, Judas, The Victim, Samadhi, The Acrobat, Mental Purity, The Law of Reversal, Baptism, The Drowned Man, The Musician, Balder, The Divine Giving-Forth, Stable Intelligence, The Redeemer in the Waters, The Old Man of the Sea, The Example, The Sacrificed God, Dissolution, Poseidon, The Dancer, The Severity of Splendour).

13 **Scorpio** – *Death* (The Grim Reaper, The Circle Completed, The Scythe, The Angel of Death, The Skeleton, The Angel Azrail, Transformation, Reincarnation, Change, Sunrise, Sex, The Tax Man, Liberation, Reproduction, The Dark Angel of the Doors, The Tunnel, The Eagle, The Child of the Great Transformation, Thanatos, Charon, Birth, The Great Snake, Kundalini, Metamorphosis, The Scorpion, Motion, Imaginative Intelligence, The Three Manifestations of Matter, The American Indian, The Red Man, The Sovereignty and Result of Victory).

14 **Sagittarius** – *Temperance* (Art, Alchemy, The Two Urns, Adaptation, The Bringer-Forth of Life, Daughter of the Reconcilers, The Teacher, The Way, Preservation, Higher Spaces, Verification, Tentative Intelligence, Intelligence of Probation or Trial, The Fourth Dimension, The Angel Michael, The Rainbow's Promise, The Pointer, The Arrow That Pierces the Rainbow, Iris, Universal Life, Consummation of the Royal Alchemical Marriage, Chiron, The Queen of Heaven, The Operation of the Great Work, The Quest of the Universal Medicine, The Coniunctio Oppositorum, Mantra, Combination, Wrath, The Beauty of a Firm Basis).

15 **Capricorn** – *Old Pan* (The Devil, The Establishment, Matter, The Cube of Imperfect Understanding, Lord of the Gates of Matter, Formless Form, Child of the Forces of Time, Typhon, The Electric Whirlwind, God as Perceived by the Ignorant, Satan, Fate, The Twins Chained by Time,

The Angel Lucifer, The Spirit of Discord, Master of the Coven, Old Nick, City Hall, The Goat of Mendes, Society, Guardian of the Key to the Temple, Janus, The Mountain, The Eye of the Father of the Temple of Universal Peace Among Men, The World Father, The Watching Eye, The Black of Ignorance, Argus of the Many Eyes, Eroticism, The Path of the Tradition of Darkness, The Scapegoat, The Clown, Opacity, Shiva, Two-Sexed Horus, Bondage, Mirth, Renewing Intelligence, The Climber, The Sovereignty and Beauty of Material Splendour).

16 **Mars** – *Tower* (The Force of Nature, Exciting Intelligence, The Fall of Adam, Crucifixion, The Cities of the Plain, Preparation Through Destruction for the New Birth, Pride of Intellect, Infatuation, Catastrophe, The Dark Night of the Soul, The Ruined Tower, The Castle of Plutus, The Column Joachim, Megalomania, The Effect, The Opening of the Eye of Shiva, The Tower of Destruction, The Fire of Heaven, The House of God, The Tower of Babel, Lord of the Hosts of the Mighty, Phallic Energy, Grace and Sin, Anger, The Red One, Awakening, The Crisis Point, The Lightning-Struck Tower, The Victory over Splendour).

17 **Aquarius** – *Star* (Star of the Magi, Sirius, Destiny, Natural Intelligence, Revelation, Meditation, Astrology, Hapi, Ganymede, Brotherhood, The Imagination of Nature, The Dog Star, The Star of Bethlehem, The Pool of Memory, Daughter of the Firmament, The Stars, Sattva, Hope, The Dweller Between the Waters, The Friend, The Group, Humanity, The Unveiling of Nature, The Supernal Power of Divine Fire, The Food of the Gods, The Grave of Death, Altruistic Love, Freedom, The Free Man, Soma, The Victory of Fundamental Strength, The Homosexual Lover).

18 **Pisces** – *Moon* (Dreams, Twilight, Dusk, The Ruler of Flux and Reflux, Child of the Sons of the Mighty, Medusa, Hecate, The Fish-God, Sleep, Body Knowledge, Trance, The Land of Dreams, Corporeal Intelligence, Organisation, The True Base of Reality, The Land of the Gods, The Gateway to Resurrection, Fantasy, The Hounds of Diana, Tamas, Music, Metaphysical Sleep, Poetry, Ast the Serpent, Basic Understanding, The Victory of the Material).

19 **The Sun** – *Sun* (Eternal Youth, Self, The Centre, Lord of the Fire of the World, Ra, The Symbol of Tetragrammaton, Apollo, The Eternal Child, Christ, Phaethon, Mithra, The Spiritual Phallus, The Central Fire, Continuous Energy, Illumination, Lord of the Aeon, Rajas, Collective Intelligence, Regeneration, Fertility and Sterility, The Splendour of Fundamental Strength).

20 **Pluto** – *Last Judgement* (Perpetual Intelligence, Realisation, Resurrection, The Day of Wrath, Vulcan, The Raising of the Dead, The One-Way Trip, The Horn, The Angel Gabriel, King of the After-Life, Hades, The Great Vocation, The Physical Phallus, Spirit of the Primal Fire, Lord of the Underworld, The Hidden One, The Apocalypse, The Swan of Leda, Shiva, Dionysiac Ecstasy, The Gangster, Rise, That Which Limits the Auric Egg, The Kidnapper, The Force of Gravity, Conscious Immortality, The Phoenix, The Splendour of the Material World).

21 **Saturn** – *World* (The Virgin Universe, The Cosmos, Aion, The Great Ones of the Night of Time, The Crown of the Magi, Kronos, The God of Fertility, The Old God, The Point of Now, Dominion or Slavery, Reality, The Esoteric Side of Nature, Immortality, The Dancing Hermaphrodite, The Centre of the Cube of Space, That Which Holds All Together, Administrative Intelligence, Cosmic Consciousness, The Initiated One, The Regents of the Earth, Guardian of the Times of Man, The Dance of Shiva, The Slain God, The Eternal Present, The Foundation of the Cosmic Elements and of the Material World).

The attributions above are in accordance with those of the Hermetic Order of the Golden Dawn, The Society of the Inner Light and the Builders of the Adytum (B.O.T.A.). I have settled on these after years of experimentation, as they seem to be verified by the human unconscious.

SUPPLEMENTAL GENERAL WORKSHEET
(for any horoscope)

Natural opposites or polarities whose balance may be checked:

Emperor and Justice (The partnership polarity)
High Priest and Death (The money-sex polarity)
Lovers and Temperance
Chariot and Old Pan (The parental polarity)
Strength and Star (The love polarity)
Hermit and Moon
Tower and Empress (The partnership polarity)
Empress and Last Judgement (The money-sex polarity)
Magician and Wheel of Fortune
High Priestess and World (The parental polarity)
Sun and Fool (The spiritual love polarity)
Magician and Hanged Man
World and Wheel of Fortune
Sun and High Priestess
Fool and Hanged Man
High Priestess and Last Judgement
Last Judgement and Magician

VRANIA   PTOLEMAEVS

Woodcut from *Textue de Sphaera* by Sacrabosco (1538).

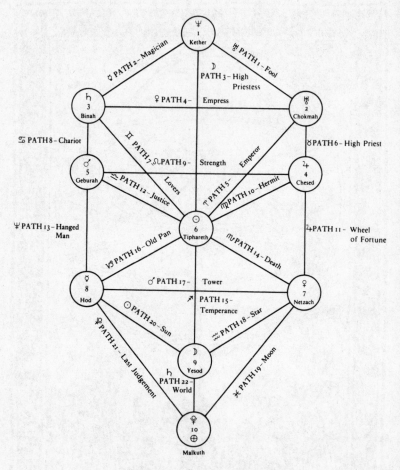

'Tree of Life' diagram.

13.
Horoscope-'Tree of Life' Sphere Equivalents and Images

1. Kether (Neptune) — An ancient bearded king seen in profile. The crown.
2. Chokmah (Uranus) — A bearded male figure. A phallus.
3. Binah (Saturn) — A mature woman. A matron. The yoni. The cup or chalice.
4. Chesed (Jupiter) — A mighty crowned and throned king.
5. Geburah (Mars) — A mighty warrior in his chariot. The sword.
6. Tiphareth (Sun) — A majestic king. A child. A sacrificed god.
7. Netzach (Venus) — A beautiful naked woman. A rose.
8. Hod (Mercury) — An hermaphrodite.
9. Yesod (Moon) — A beautiful naked man, very strong.
10. Malkuth (Earth and Pluto) — A young woman, crowned and throned.

4

CHESED

'Tree of Life' Sphere *Chesed* from the D.O.M.E. Meditation Cards by Sheila W. Ross.

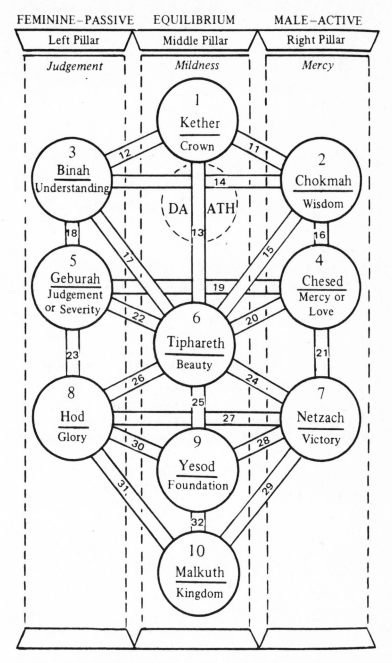

FEMININE–PASSIVE   EQUILIBRIUM   MALE–ACTIVE

Left Pillar   Middle Pillar   Right Pillar

Judgement   *Mildness*   *Mercy*

1
Kether
Crown

3
Binah
Understanding

2
Chokmah
Wisdom

DA ATH

5
Geburah
Judgement
or Severity

4
Chesed
Mercy or
Love

6
Tiphareth
Beauty

8
Hod
Glory

7
Netzach
Victory

9
Yesod
Foundation

10
Malkuth
Kingdom

Diagram of the 'Tree of Life' showing the 32 Paths.

14.

Example Worksheet

(Horoscope translated into tarot archetypes):

Edwin Charles Steinbrecher, April 4, 1930, 10.55 p.m. CST, Chicago, Illinois, U.S.A.

High Energy Relationships	Check Union Between:
Temperance and Lovers (Twins)	High Priestess and Sun
Magician and World	High Priestess and Magician
Magician and Last Judgement	High Priestess and Empress
Sun and World	High Priestess and Hanged Man
Sun and Last Judgement	Magician and Sun
Tower and Wheel of Fortune	Magician and Tower
World and Fool	Magician and Wheel of Fortune
World and Last Judgement	Magician and Fool
Fool and Last Judgement	Sun and Wheel of Fortune
Emperor and Justice	Sun and Fool
Chariot and Old Pan (Devil)	Tower and World
Hermit and Moon	Wheel of Fortune and World
Strength and Star	Wheel of Fortune and Fool
Death and High Priest (Hierophant)	Wheel of Fortune and Last Judgement

Basic Archetypes:

Sun   Magician
Tower of Fortune   Moon
Hanged Man   Hermit
World   Old Pan
Wheel of Fortune   Lovers
Emperor

**First Questions to
Archetypes (with Guide):**

1. What do you need from me and from my life to work with me and be my friend? 2. What do you have to give me that I need from you? (Ask for a symbolic object, its interpretation as to what it represents, its powers and uses as a tool, and where in the body to absorb and carry it.)

Circle of Hands with:

1. Hermit, Temperance, Moon and Lovers

2. World, Fool, Sun, Magician and Last Judgement
3. Justice, Old Pan, Emperor and Chariot
4. Strength, Death, Star and High Priest
5. Shadow man
6. High Energy and Union pairs
7. Basic Archetypes

Consciousness Resistant Factors:

Empress   Death
Wheel of Fortune   Lovers
High Priestess   Hermit
Hanged Man

'Alien' Energy Contructs:

Uranian *Power* = Fool + Sun + Magician + Emperor + Empress (male figure)
Fixed Adept = High Priest + Strength + Death + Star (male or female figure)

CARDINAL T-CROSS ENERGY BALANCING CONSTRUCT

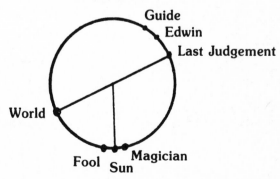

15.
Example Horoscope

Uranian <u>Power</u>
<u>Fixed</u> Adept

Cardinal T-Cross
Aries Stellium

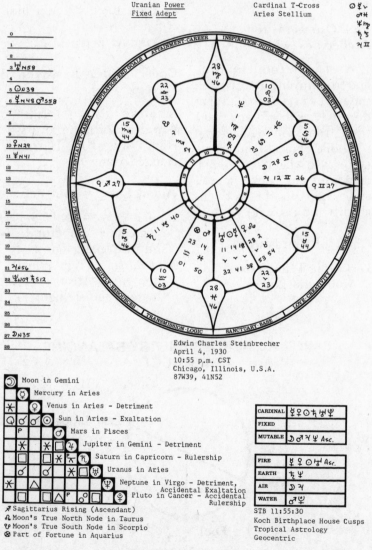

Edwin Charles Steinbrecher
April 4, 1930
10:55 p.m. CST
Chicago, Illinois, U.S.A.
87W39, 41N52

☽ Moon in Gemini
☿ Mercury in Aries
♀ Venus in Aries - Detriment
☉ Sun in Aries - Exaltation
♂ Mars in Pisces
♃ Jupiter in Gemini - Detriment
♄ Saturn in Capricorn - Rulership
♅ Uranus in Aries
♆ Neptune in Virgo - Detriment, Accidental Exaltation
♇ Pluto in Cancer - Accidental Rulership

♐ Sagittarius Rising (Ascendant)
☊ Moon's True North Node in Taurus
☋ Moon's True South Node in Scorpio
⊗ Part of Fortune in Aquarius

CARDINAL	☿ ♀ ☉ ♄ ♅ ♆
FIXED	
MUTABLE	☽ ♂ ♃ ♆ Asc.

FIRE	☿ ♀ ☉ ♅ Asc.
EARTH	♄ ♆
AIR	☽ ♃
WATER	♂ ♇

STB 11:55:30
Koch Birthplace House Cusps
Tropical Astrology
Geocentric

Example horoscope.

16.

How to Plug Your Relatives into Your Horoscope

One's relatives may be 'plugged in' to one's natal horoscope where they may be seen as outer aspects of specific areas of one's life. They will function as *barometers* of these areas. For this it is useful to discover the correct pregnancy or fathering order of your relatives' (mother's, father's, grandmothers', brothers', sisters', aunts', sisters-in-law's, mothers-in-law's, etc.) pregnancies or children fathered. Try to obtain this information as accurately as possible. Miscarriages and abortions each count as a pregnancy, and *where*, not when, they occurred in the birth sequence is important. Twins count as two pregnancies, and which twin was first-born is important. By barometers I mean that the indicated relatives *as their ego personalities are perceived by you* (how they react to and handle the events in their lives in your eyes) will function to show you how you are handling that area of your own life for which they stand as a symbol. To be a barometer has only to do with how *you* judge them to be dealing with their lives, not their own evaluation of themselves and their lives nor the evaluations of others reported to you.

The 'building block' roles are *mother, father, child, sibling* (brother or sister) and *partner*. With these five basic role concepts every person related to you through blood, role or law can be put into one specific area of your personal pattern – relatives as distant as third cousins on your mother's side or great-great-aunts on your father's side.

Father is always a 10th House role. So the father of any person in your horoscope through your perception of his role relationship will always be the 10th House from the House which the person himself is. For instance, *the child of your mother's first pregnancy not counting you* will be your first sibling (your first brother or sister). This sibling will correspond to

Original Tarot Trump of *The High Priestess* based on ancient gypsy packs by Basil Ivan Rakacsi

your 3rd House. (In other words the 1st House or Ascendant of your first brother or sister in your horoscope will be your 3rd House.) Then the 10th House from the 3rd, your 12th House, will be the relationship you will perceive between your first sibling and your father. Your perception of your father and the behaviour *you*, not your brothers or sisters, draw out of him will be described by your 10th House as the father's 1st House or Ascendant. If you turn the horoscope so that the 10th House becomes an Ascendant, the twelve House horoscope you will be looking at will describe your father, his actions and behaviours and what happens to him in your reality. It can be read in the same way as if it were his actual horoscope, but only in your reality perception, not necessarily his own. Your 11th House then becomes his 2nd, your 12th House, his 3rd, etc. So mother's father will be your 1st House, your first child's relationship to its father in your eyes will be your 2nd House, your father's father will be your 7th House, etc.

The role of **Mother** is always a 4th House relationship, so your 4th House as your own mother's Ascendant or 1st House will indicate to you her actions and behaviours in your personal reality. Hence, your mother's mother will be your 7th House, your father's mother, your 1st House (or ego barometer), your first child's relationship to mother, your 8th House (the 4th House from the 5th) etc.

Sibling is always a 3rd House relationship. So your first sibling will be the 3rd House from the 1st House or your 3rd House. Your second sibling will be the 3rd House from the 3rd House or your 5th House. The third sibling, the 3rd House from the 5th House or the 7th House, etc. Your father's first sibling will be the 3rd House from the 10th House, so your first aunt or uncle on your father's side will be described by your 12th House as that aunt's or uncle's Ascendant or 1st House. (Remember to check for miscarriages, abortions and stillborn children or children born out of wedlock in all birth sequences.) The second aunt or uncle on your father's side will then be your 2nd House, the third, your 4th House, etc.

Child is always a 5th House relationship, so the first child you father or conceive will have your 5th House as his or her Ascendant. The next child, the sibling, or brother or sister, of your first child, will be your 7th House (the 3rd House from the 5th), the third child, your 9th House, etc. Remember to count *each pregnancy,* whether the child was miscarried, aborted, given away, stillborn or born, as one slot. Say that your first pregnancy, or the first pregnancy you fathered was a set of fraternal twins, a girl, first-born, and a boy, second-born. Then the daughter would be your 5th House and the son, your 7th House. Your father's first sibling's first child by the same rule would be your 4th House (the 5th House of the 12th). Your partner's first child by a previous marriage would be your 11th House (the 5th House of the 7th), and should you legally adopt this child before you have any children of your own, the child would transfer to your 5th House. If you already had two children, the adopted son or daughter would become your 9th House.

Partner, whether business or marriage, where it is a relationship of shared responsibility (this includes roommates and those you live with while you are living with them, all ex-partners, all persons you have contractual agreements with, and anyone you have impregnated or conceived a child by whether the child was born or not), is a 7th House relationship. So your mother's partner (father or step-father) is your 10th House, the 7th House from the 4th. Your partner is the 7th House, the 7th House from the 1st. Your first child's partner is the 11th House, the 7th or opposite House from the 5th. Your father's first sibling's partner, your aunt or uncle by marriage, becomes your 6th House, the 7th House from the 12th.

The following horoscope diagram gives a smattering of what each of the astrological Houses of life areas describes, as well as examples of some of the relatives which fall into each. I have included automobiles as barometers, because we have so many of them in our culture. Cars are always a 3rd House relationship (like siblings), as is any vehicle (as the mind is the vehicle of the ego or Ascendant). In lieu of a car, a bicycle, tricycle or just experiences encountered while walking will serve the 3rd House function.

The males and females in the same House as barometers may not seem at all the same in the eyes of the ego, although the men will resemble each other as will the women. Each will serve to indicate to the individual how his male and female energies in the area being focused on are being handled. For instance in the 7th House, if the wife seems in very good shape but the third sibling, who is a brother, seems in bad shape, it would indicate that the feminine or *yin* energies in that life area are being assimilated into consciousness but the masculine energies are not. Working with the masculine facets of that life arena in the Inner Guide Meditation, will produce a positive change in the brother as you, the ego, bring the more *yang* aspects of your 7th House into the light of consciousness.

We are all connected, one to the other, by *projection*. This projection, the two-way energy flow which connects us all, produces real action and behaviour in others who take roles in our realities. Those you project on are also projecting onto you, but until you *experience* how your energies are manipulating the other's life you will never understand how you receive and live out the projections of another.

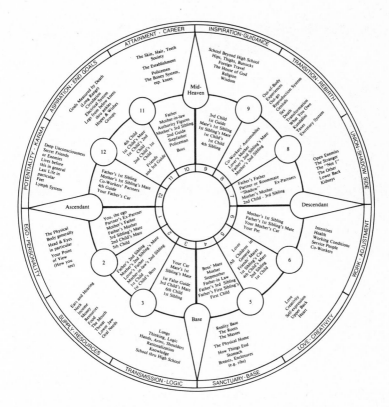

Horoscope diagram: Elements having to do with each of the twelve houses of the horoscope.

Again, for all practical purposes, *there's no one out there but aspects of yourself* that are being projected on everyone and everything. Once you make yourself more conscious, your entire reality and everyone in it becomes more conscious.

17.

Famous 'Aliens'

The following people, famous and infamous, are given here, because they are people in the public eye or historical figures whose lives can be followed in the newspapers or periodicals or researched in biographies, autobiographies and history books. Thus, these examples enable those with similar 'Alien' constructs to see how other individuals have dealt with these specialized forces and patterns in their lives.

The Alien Powers (Sun in Conjunction with Saturn, Uranus, Neptune or Pluto)

The **Powers** have a high priest function in either a male or female body. Specialized energy radiates and extends from them out into their environments affecting whomever it touches. The effects on others take place whether or not the individual **Powers** have consciousness of the energy they carry.

The Saturnian **Powers** are the masters of time, space, dimension, government, history, form, permanence, structure, humour and the secrets of geometry and natural law as it functions on the Earth plane. They have innate knowledge of the energies produced, transmitted or contained in three dimensional forms. Their energy brings to form and stabilizes whomever they are with, and they have the ability to accurately visualize and build anything. They are the oldest of the Aliens, having manifested in humankind as soon as awareness of the solar system and its movements occurred in human consciousness. They function as the testers and guardians of humanity. Resistance to consciousness of their abilities takes the forms of rigidity, feelings of inferiority, aloofness, work-oholicism, depression, despair, marijuana addiction, uptightness, anxiety, judgementalness, ennui, power-tripping, mono-level awareness, apathy, loneliness, fear, paranoia, grandiosity and a general separation from the All in word and deed.

Saturnian Powers – Hank Aaron, Conrad Aiken, Pope Alexander VI, Jack Anderson, Ann-Margret, Eve Arden, W. H. Auden, John Logie Baird, Faith Baldwin, Kay Ballard, Alan Bates, Pierre Charles Baudelaire, Warren Beatty, Philip Berrigan, St. Bernadette of Lourdes, Leonard Bernstein, Rudolph Bing, Helena Blavatsky, Ray Bradbury, Tycho Brahe, Rupert Brooke, Jerry Brown, Jim Brown, William F. Buckley, Jr., Richard Burton, Richard Carlson, Billy Carter, Roger Chaffee, Marc Chagall, Marge Champion, Otis Chandler, Raymond Chandler, Cheiro, Julie Christie, Jim Clark, Colette, Perry Como, Robert Conrad, Francis Ford Coppola, Richard Crenna, Xavier Cugat, e.e. cummings, Marie Curie, Dante Alighieri, Linda Darnell, Bette Davis, Olivia DeHavilland, Marlene Dietrich, Albert Dürer, Albert Einstein, Mircea Eliade, Alice Faye, Father Edward Flanagan, Stephen Collins Foster, Emperor Franz Joseph of Austria, David Frost, Mary Garden, George VI of England, Cary Grant, Ulysses S. Grant, D. W. Griffith, H. Rider Haggard, Rex Harrison, Huntington Hartford, Franz Hartmann, Franz Joseph Haydn, Florence Henderson, O. Henry, Paul Hindemith, Elbert Hubbard, Rock Hudson, William James, Robert Joffrey, James Earl Jones, Scott Joplin, Winnie Ruth Judd, Herbert von Karajan, Robert F. Kennedy, Deborah Kerr, Piper Laurie, T. E. Lawrence, Alan Leo, Richard Lester, Charles Lloyd, Jack Lord, H. P. Lovecraft, Amy Lowell, Martin Luther, Sue Lyon, Balyoge Shawar Maharaji-Ji, Lee Majors, Jayne Mansfield, Margarethe of Denmark, W. Somerset Maugham, Robin Moore, Grandma Moses, Wolfgang Amadeus Mozart, Sheree North, Rudolf Nureyev, Annie Oakley, Sean O'Casey, Odetta, Juan Peron, Wendell Phillips, Isaac Pitman, Pope Pius XII, François Rabelais, Michael Redgrave, Jerry Reed, Christopher Reeve, Lance Reventlow, Richard III of England, Sigmund Romberg, Linda Ronstadt, Mickey Rooney, Camille Saint-Saëns, Arthur Schopenhauer, Sir Walter Scott, Alexander Scriabin, Bugsy Siegal, Phil Silvers, Kate Smith, Sam Snead, Julie Sommars, Baruch Spinoza, Sylvester Stallone, Gertrude Stein, Margaret Sullavan, Joan Sutherland, Nikola Tesla, St Thérèse of Lisieux, Bobby Unser, Jack Valenti, Mamie Van

Doren, George Wallace, Franz Werfel, James Whitmore, Robert Anton Wilson, Jonathan Winters, Sulamith Wülfing, Jamie Wyeth.

The Uranian Powers are the masters of freedom, altruistic love, astrology, electricity and all vibratory phenomena, invention, innovation and group process. They tend to have little understanding of normal human time, see tomorrow more easily than today, and bring forth projects and ideas that are generally seven years ahead of the rest of humanity, if not more. They have what is called 'instant empathy', generating in others the feeling that the other person has known them forever – that they are old friends and confidants, beyond time. They have few, if any, of the normal prejudices of the world and can even forget what sex, religion or colour another person is, relating always to the person's real essence. They are non-judgemental and are often considered to have genius because of their abilities to perceive innate patterns in things and situations, and because of their multi-level awareness. Their job is to make sure that natural law on Earth conforms to and changes with Universal law. They are the illusion breakers, and they free locked-in conditions and destroy outmoded forms. They have elements of surprise and unpredictability in their behaviours. They, along with the Plutonians, are masters of the release and control of the Kundalini energy or Serpent Power which sleeps at the base of the human spine. Resistance to consciousness of their abilities takes the forms of rebelliousness, iconoclasm, flakiness, lawlessness, chaos, coldness, antisocial behaviours, revolution, reporting the ideal instead of the real, anarchy, electrical overcharges in their bodies and acute nervousness.

Uranian Powers – Chas Adams, Edward Albee, Dana Andrews, Queen Anne of England, Eddie Arcaro, Lucie Arnaz, Charles Atlas, Lew Ayres, Diana Barrymore, Ethel Barrymore, L. Frank Baum, Simone de Beauvoir, David Ben-Gurion, Shelley Berman, Neils Bohr, Victor Borge, Frank Borman, Pierre Boulez, Fanny Brice, Helen Gurley Brown, Beau Brummell, Carol Burnett, William Burroughs, Admiral Richard E. Byrd, Erskine Caldwell, Glen Campbell, Paul Foster Case, Catherine de Medicis of France, Cyd Charisse, Gary Collins, Judy Collins, John Constable, Le Corbusier, Samuel Dash, Rennie Davis, Sandy Dennis, Walt Disney, Helen Gahagan Douglas, Hugh Downs, Sir Arthur Conan

Doyle, Alexandre Dumas, Irene Dunne, Arni Egilsson, John Ehrlichman, Dwight D. Eisenhower, T. S. Eliot, Farouk of Egypt, Reshád Feild, Zsa Zsa Gabor, John Gavin, Llewellyn George, Vitas Gerulaitis, Emma Goldman, Barry Goldwater, Samuel Goldwyn, Peter Graves, Lorne Greene, Joel Grey, Charles Grodin, Dorothy Hamill, Mata Hari, Bruno Hauptmann, Werner Heisenberg, Justice Oliver Wendell Holmes, Winslow Homer, Herbert Hoover, Jean Houston, Howard Hughes, Glenda Jackson, David Janssen, St Joan of Arc, Jennifer Jones, Marc Edmund Jones, Carl G. Jung, Danny Kaye, Stacey Keach, Johannes Kepler, Jack Kerouac, Gareth Knight, Gene Krupa, Jesse L. Lasky, Anton Szandor LaVey, D. H. Lawrence, Sybil Leek, Oscar Levant, Jerry Lewis, William Lily, John Locke, Joseph Losey, James Lovell, George Lucas, Ida Lupino, Shirley MacLaine, Stéphane Mallarmé, Herbie Mann, Katherine Mansfield, John P. Marquand, Carson McCullers, Rod McKuen, Aimee Semple McPherson, Steve McQueen, Margaret Mead, Zubin Mehta, Dame Nellie Melba, H. L. Mencken, Ray Milland, Elizabeth Montgomery, Thomas Moore, Jack Nicholson, Leonard Nimoy, Richard M. Nixon, Justice Sandra Day O'Connor, Andres Pollard Ogg, Eugene O'Neill, Eugene Ormandy, Empress Farah Diba Pahlavi of Iran, Jack Palance, Maxfield Parrish, Pier Paolo Pasolini, Tony Perkins, Pope Pius XI, George Plimpton, Jackson Pollack, Marcel Proust, Luise Rainer, Ramakrishna, Ram Dass, James Earl Ray, John Reed, Django Reinhardt, Pierre-Auguste Renoir, Debbie Reynolds, Nikolai Rimsky-Korsakov, Mary Roberts Rinehart, Pete Rozelle, Otis Rush, Walter Schirra, Ronald Searle, Omar Sharif, William Shatner, Ted Shawn, Sidney Sheldon, Mary Shelley, Percy Bysshe Shelley, Stephen Sondheim, Joe Sorrentino, Ann sothern, Richard Strauss, St Teresa of Avila, Theodora Van Runkle, Erich Von Däniken, Erich Von Stroheim, Arthur Wellesley (Duke of Wellington), Simon Wiesenthal, William Butler Yeats, Emperor Yoshihito Taisho Tenno of Japan, Roger Zelazny, Ron Ziegler.

The Neptunian Powers are the masters of magnetism, mysticism, illusion, invisibility, compassion and the archetypal reality levels. They dissolve things and situations no longer useful to the planet's evolution. They are the sensitives and the psychics. Their love is pure compassion, because they are able to perceive the common thread that connects all things. They are the illusion makers, because they are also the masters of the process now understood as psychological projection. They are the knowers of movements and dances that reflect and draw into the Earth plane energies and patterns of the Universe from other reality dimensions. They are natural musicians, poets, dancers, film makers, clairvoyants, mystics and weavers of fantasies. Information comes to them in feeling and picture, and they feel everything, like raw nerves in the world. Resistance to consciousness of their abilities takes the forms of spaciness, supersensitivity, seduction, deception, fears of the unreal, absentmindedness, letting themselves be victimized, escapism, addiction, degeneracy, delusion, dissipation, gullibility, wishful thinking, weakness, impracticality and isolation from others. All the Neptune Aliens need periodic physical privacy in order to stay centered.

Neptunian Powers – A. E., Brian Aldiss, Horatio Alger, George Arliss, Louis Armstrong, Frankie Avalon, James Baldwin, Anne Bancroft, Lionel Barrymore, Sir Thomas Beecham, Vincenzo Bellini, Tony Bennett, Milton Berle, Ann Blyth, William Jennings Bryan, William Cullen Bryant, James Branch Cabell, Rory Calhoun, Rosalyn Carter, Fidel Castro, Paul Cézanne, George Chakiris, Charles V of France, Chubby Checker, Lord Randolph Churchill, Eldridge Cleaver, Patsy Cline, James Coburn, Sean Connery, Mike Connors, Emile Coué, Robert Culp, Gabriele D'Anunzio, Dino DeLaurentis, John Derek, Vittorio DeSica, Rudolf Diesel, Gustave Doré, Mike Douglas, Sir Alec Douglas-Home, Nelson Eddy, Mama Cass Elliot, Desiderius Erasmus, Werner Erhardt, Carrie Fisher, Eddie Fisher, Pat Flanagan, Gerald R. Ford, Jr., Leif Garrett, David Garroway, Ben Gazzara, Rudi Gernreich, Ellen Glasgow, Maxim Gorky, Kenneth Grahame, Alex Haley, George Frederick Handel, Robert Heinlein, Sir Edmund Hillary, Hedda Hopper, Harry Houdini, A. E. Housman, James II of England, John I of England, Al Jolson, John Keats, Ken Kesey, Sidney Lanier, Charles Laughton, William Powell Lear, Anton van Leeuwenhoek, Art Linkletter, Henry Cabot Lodge, Sophia Loren, Guglielmo Marconi, Princess Margaret Rose of England, William McKinley, Don McLean, Marshall McLuhan, Ashley Montagu, Claudio Monteverdi, Bob Newhart, Donald O'Connor, Clifford Odets, Maureen O'Hara, Sidney Omarr, George Orwell, Debra Paget, Mark Phillips, Ira Progoff, Sergei Rachmaninoff, Erick Maria Remarque, Prince Zoorosh Ali Reza of Iran, Nelson Rockefeller, Gene Roddenberry, Richard Rodgers, Ginger Rogers, Jimmy Rogers, Rose Marie, Edmond Rostand, Peter Paul Rubens, Antoine de Saint-Exupéry, George Sanders, Sepharial, Wallis Simpson (Duchess of Windsor), A. P. Sinnett, Red Skelton, Suzanne Somers, Barbara Stanwyck, Charles Proteus Steinmetz, Isaac Stern, Terry Thomas, Lily Tomlin, Arturo Toscanini, Leon Uris, Jan Vermeer, Raquel Welch, Esther Williams, Shelley Winters, Hugo Wolf, Jo Anne Worley, Sir Christopher Wren, Wilbur Wright.

The Plutonian Powers are the masters of metamorphosis and irreversible change. They move things and situations from one level of being to the next one above it, often using the acceleration of time or vibration to accomplish this. They destroy the old and outmoded through silent, relentless, often invisible, processes. They have knowledge of the workings of levitation, out-of-the-body experiences (astral projection), sex energy and the physics of sex, birth, death and rebirth. They have an innate understanding of the force called gravity, and they, with the Uranians, have to do with the release and control of the Kundalini energy, the evolutionary energy in humankind. They are the natural remodelers of the universe and have great powers and abilities relating to working with the masses because of their tremendous charismatic qualities. They are natural sleuths and finders of hidden or lost things. Resistance to consciousness of their abilities takes the forms of compulsions, murderous rage, vengefulness, sex without love, annihilation, rape, atrocities, criminal acts, depravity, debauchery, venereal disease, terrorism, sadism, sarcasm and stubborn blindness.

Plutonian Powers – John Adams, Aly Khan, Don Ameche, Paul Anka, Jean Anouilh, Sir James M. Barrie, Polly Bergen, William Blake, Bill Blass, Vida Blue, Peter Bogdanovich, Richard Boone, Margaret Bourke-White, Julian Bream, Arthur Bremer, David Brinkley, Elizabeth Barrett Browning, Yul Brynner, Bernard Buffet, Sir Richard Burton, Dick Button, Lord Byron, Pierre Cardin, Leslie Caron, Benvenuto Cellini, Bennett Cerf, Gower Champion, Frédéric Chopin, Van Cliburn, Bill Cosby, Jacques Cousteau, Bob Crane, John Crow, Robert Cummings, Clarence Darrow, Honoré Daumier, Isadore Duncan, Vince Edwards, Peggy Fleming, Errol Flynn, Harrison Ford, Anatole France, François II of France, Galilei Galileo, Farley Granger, Merv Griffin, Susan Hayward, William

Randolph Hearst, Nicky Hilton, Bob Hope, Lena Horne, Victor Hugo, Henrik Ibsen, Burl Ives, Mick Jagger, Henry James, Elisabeth Kúbler-Ross, Ann Landers, Steve Lawrence, Janet Leigh, Pope Leo XIII, Joseph Lister, Gina Lollobrigida, Henry Wadsworth Longfellow, Jeanette MacDonald, Dean Martin, Robert S. McNamera, J. Pierpoint Morgan, Sr., John Muir, Audie Murphy, Cardinal John Henry Newman, Czar Nicholas II of Russia, Jay Waverly North, Eleanor Parker, Troy Perry, Henri Philippe Petain, Della Reese, Jerry Rubin, Bertrand Russell, Jane Russel, Rosalind Russel, Susan St James, Yves Saint Laurent, Eric Satie, Martin Sheen, Oswald Spengler, Leland Stanford, Maureen Stapleton, Stendahl, Donald Sutherland, Algernon Swinburne, Rabindranath Tagore, Billy Joe Thomas, Abigail Van Buren, Andreas Vesalius, Johny Weissmuller, T. H. White, Natalie Wood, Yevgeny Yevtushenko, Emile Zola.

The Mixed **Powers** are those individuals who have two or more of the planets (Saturn, Uranus, Neptune or Pluto) in Conjunction with their Suns. They have the innate abilities of each of the planetary factors.

Mixed Powers: ● Saturn and Uranus – Paul Brunton, Noel Coward, Bob Dylan, Mamie Eisenhower, Emmet Kelly, C. S. Lewis, Joe Namath, Ricky Nelson, Ritchie Valens. ● Saturn and Neptune – Alexander Graham Bell, Luther Burbank, Pierre de Teilhard de Chardin, Buffalo Bill Cody, Phyllis Diller, Thomas Alva Edison, Charles W. Leadbeater, Robert Mitchum, Alfred de Musset, Patti Reagan, George Shearing, Louis Comfort Tiffany. ● Saturn and Pluto – Norman Cousins, Arnold Schwarzenegger, Sally Struthers. ● Uranus and Neptune – Clara Barton, Lewis Carroll, Wilkie Collins, Gustave Flaubert, General Charles Gordon, Edouard Manet, Louis Pasteur, Risë Stevens. ● Uranus and Pluto – Oliver Cromwell, René Descartes, M. C. Escher, Sigmund Freud, Grant Lewi, Anne Morrow Lindbergh, Peter Pears, Robert E. Peary, Katherine Anne Porter, Joseph Pulitzer, Paul Verlaine. ● Neptune and Pluto – Eric Ambler, Ralph Bellamy, Irving Berlin, John Dillinger, Anthony Eden, Lillian Hellman, Guy Lombardo, Norman Vincent Peale, Cole Porter, Basil Rathbone, Jean Paul Sartre, George Szell, Harry S. Truman, Immanuel Velikovsky. ● Saturn, Uranus and Pluto – Edwin Markham. ● Saturn, Neptune and Pluto – Douglas Fairbanks, Sr., Henry J. Kaiser, Andrew Wyeth.

The Alien Vessels (Moon in Conjunction with Saturn, Uranus, Neptune or Pluto)

The Vessels have the ability to draw specialized energies out of those around them, bringing these into consciousness in others through the selective magnetism they carry. They are able to receive or take through themselves specific energies from others and return these as heightened, more conscious energy forms. These effects take place in others whether or not the individual Vessels have consciousness of their magnetic effect on others. They function as 'doors' to other spaces. Theirs is a high priestess function in either a female or a male body.

The Saturnian Vessels stabilize and bring to form those they are with. They inspire practical, Earth plane ideas in others. They bring to consciousness knowledge of time, space, dimension, government, history, form, permanence, structure, humour and the secrets of geometry and natural law in others through their magnetism. They also inspire knowledge of the energies produced, transmitted and contained in three dimensional forms, especially crystals. The Saturnian Vessels along with all the other Saturn Aliens are the oldest of the Aliens on the Earth plane. Resistance to consciousness of their abilities takes on the same forms as in the Saturnian Powers, but in addition can project these forms onto those around them.

Saturnian Vessels – Herb Alpert, Jack Anderson, Neil Armstrong, James Arness, Jane Austen, Simone de Beauvoir, Melvin Belli, Rudolph Bing, Vida Blue, Frank Borman, Werner von Braun, Fanny Brice, Charlotte Brontë, George Bush, Dick Button, Truman Capote, Leslie Caron, Jimmy Carter, Enrico Caruso, Joan Crawford, Xavier Cugat, Tony Curtis, John Dewey, Khigh Dhiegh, Comtesse Du Barry, John Foster Dulles, Isadore Duncan, Eleanora Duse, Chris Evert, Manuel de Falla, Stephen Collins Foster, François II of France, Emperor Franz Joseph of Austria, Frederick the Great, Farley Granger, Cary Grant, Mata Hari, Jean Harlow, William Randolph Hearst, Hermann Hesse, Jimmy Hoffa, Marilyn Horne, Hubert H. Humphrey, Alan Jardine, Marc Edmund Jones, John Keats, Ethel Kennedy, Henry Kissinger, Sandy Koufax, Louis S. B. Leakey, Fernand Leger, John V. Lindsay, Sophia Loren, Guy Madison, Henri Matisse, Willie Mays,

William McKinley, Aimee Semple McPherson, Liza Minnelli, Prince Naruhito of Japan, Ramon Navarro, Troy Perry, Bishop James Pike, Elvis Presley, Vincent Price, Alexander Pushkin, Bhagwan Shree Rajneesh, Alain Resnais, Rainer Maria Rilke, Peter Paul Rubens, Rosalind Russell, Jean Paul Sartre, Stephen Sondheim, Rudolph Steiner, Joan Sutherland, Leigh Taylor-Young, Richard Thomas, Arturo Toscanini, Jon Voight, George Wallace, Dennis Weaver, Johny Weissmuller, James Whitmore, Hank Williams.

The Uranian Vessels draw freedom and altruistic love out of those around them. Their presence in a group allows the group to function in a friendly, cooperative way. They inspire ideas relating to astrology, vibratory phenomena, invention, innovation and the avant garde in others. They are friendly, non-judgemental and have few prejudices, if any. They have the ability to free the Kundalini or any other blocked energy in others. Resistance to consciousness of their abilities takes on the same forms as in the Uranian Powers, but in addition they can project these forms into those around them.

Uranian Vessels – Eddie Albert, Sr., Louisa May Alcott, Ann-Margret, Max Baer, John Baez, Jim Bailey, Sarah Bernhardt, Tycho Brahe, William F. Buckley, Jr., Ellen Burstyn, Lord Byron, Edith Cavell, Paul Cézanne, Georges Clemenceau, Jackie Coogan, James Fenimore Cooper, Sir William Crookes, Dante Alighieri, Gustave Doré, Dwight D. Eisenhower, Keith Emerson, Peter Frampton, Ava Gardner, George III of England, J. Paul Getty, Arthur Godfrey, Hermann Göring, Brett Harte, Goldie Hawn, Herbert Hoover, Ken Howard, Leslie Howard, Barbara Hutton, Mick Jagger, Jinarajadasa, Jim Jones, Rockwell Kent, Timothy Leary, Vivien Leigh, Charles Lindbergh, Guy Lombardo, Jack London, H. P. Lovecraft, Bob Mackie, Mary Martin, Eugene McCarthy, General George B. McClellan, Meher Baba, Henry Miller, John Milton, Grandma Moses, Ricky Nelson, Anais Nin, Sergei Prokofiev, Joachim von Ribbentrop, Nikolai Rimsky-Korsakov, Max Roach, Gene Roddenberry, Eric Satie, George Bernard Shaw, David Shire, Red Skelton, Joseph Stalin, Emmanuel Swedenborg, Gene Tierney, Lana Turner, Roger Vadim, Edgar Varèse, Barbara Villiers (Lady Castlemaine), Orson Welles, John Wesley, Wendell Wilkie.

The Neptunian Vessels draw compassion and deep mystical feelings from others. They inspire knowledge relating to magnetism, illusion, the psychic, invisibility and the archetypal reality levels in others. They are sensitive and profoundly psychic, their psychic information coming to them in feeling and picture. Those around them also become more psychic and visionary. They draw information about music, poetry dance and film from those around them. Resistance to consciousness of their abilities takes on the same forms as with the Neptunian Powers, but in addition they can project these forms into those around them.

Neptunian Vessels – Konrad Adenauer, Brian Aldiss, Maxwell Anderson, Johann Sebastian Bach, Hector Berlioz, Lenny Bruce, Corinne Calvet, Andrew Carnegie, Princess Caroline of Monaco, Scott Carpenter, Miguel de Cervantes, James Clavell, Robert Cummings, Charles Dickens, Elizabeth II of England, Zelda Fitzgerald, Errol Flynn, Ann Frank, Leif Garrett, Graham Greene, Joan Hackett, Franz Hartmann, Franz Joseph Haydn, Dustin Hoffman, William Holden, A. E. Housman, Stacey Keach, Edward M. Kennedy, Johannes Kepler, Billie Jean King, Evel Knievel, Hedy Lamarr, Gypsy Rose Lee, Jack Lemmon, C. S. Lewis, Anne Morrow Lindbergh, Charles Lloyd, Henry Cabot Lodge, Shirley MacLaine, Michael Nesmith, George Orwell, Marcel Proust, Raphael of Urbino, Robert Redford, Django Reinhardt, Jimmy Rogers, Albert Schweitzer, Talia Shire, Ian Smith, Robert Louis Stevenson, Booth Tarkington, Margaret Thatcher, Spencer Tracy, Pierre Trudeau, Peter Ustinov, Gloria Vanderbilt, Gwen Verdon, Simone Weil, Edward White, Jr., Jamie Wyeth.

The Plutonian Vessels draw transformation energy from others. They inspire knowledge relating to sexuality, the Kundalini or transformation process, astral projection, levitation, birth and death. They have the ability to free the Kundalini or any other blocked energy in others, hence their healing powers are great. Resistance to consciousness of their abilities takes on the same forms as in the Plutonian Powers, but in addition they can unconsciously project these forms into those around themselves and not see them in themselves.

Plutonian Vessels – John Quincy Adams, Eddie Albert, Jr., Desi Arnaz, Jr., Fred Astaire, Rona Barrett, Sir Max Beerbohm, Shelley Berman, Timothy Bottoms, Charles Boyer, Jerry Brown, John Cage, Roger Chaffee, Cyd Charisse, Charles II of Engand, Van Cliburn, Mike Connors, Honoré Daumier, Adelle Davis, Bette Davis, Doris Day, John Dee, Phyllis Diller,

Dr Tom Dooley, Faye Dunaway, Lawrence Durrell, Arni Egilsson, Pat Flanagan, Larry Flynt, Harrison Ford, Mary Garden, Kenneth Grahame, Kathryn Grayson, Sir Alec Guinness, H. R. Haldeman, O. Henry, Olivia Hussey, Carl G. Jung, Herbert von Karajan, Elisabeth Kübler-Ross, Princess Margaret Rose of England, Paul McCartney, Edgar Dean Mitchell, Marcia Moore, Wolfgang Amadeus Mozart, Willie Nelson, Jay Waverly North, Clifford Odets, Wendell Phillips, Pope Pius XII, Edgar Allan Poe, Dan Rather, Pierre-Auguste Renoir, Richard II of England, Oral Roberts, Walter Reuther, Eric Sevareid, Martin Sheen, Phoebe Snow, Julie Sommars, Maureen Stapleton, Ringo Starr, James Stewart, Johann Strauss, Barbara Streisand, Algernon Swinburne, Lee Trevino, Mark Twain, Twiggy, Theodora Van Runkle, Robert Wagner, Ted Williams, Emile Zola.

Mixed Vessels: ● Saturn and Uranus – A. J. Cronin, Bob Dylan, Art Garfunkel, George VI of England. ● Saturn and Neptune – Jacques Bergerac, Susan Hayward, Franz Liszt. ● Saturn and Pluto – David Bowie, Moyshe Dyan, Rollie Fingers, Benito Mussolini. ● Uranus and Neptune – Francis Galton, Herman Melville. ● Uranus and Pluto – Oliver Cromwell, Anatole France. ● Neptune and Pluto – Don Ameche, Jack Benny, Edgar Cayce, Le Corbusier, Noel Coward, Amelia Earhart, Max Ernst, Francisco Franco, Fulcanelli, Colleen Moore, Mary Pickford, David O. Selznick, Lotte von Strahl, Walter Winchell.

The Alien Instruments (Saturn, Uranus, Neptune or Pluto in the First House of the Horoscope or in Conjunction with the Ascendant from the Twelfth House)

The Instruments amplify the energy they carry in those around them, e.g. the Neptunian Instruments making those around them more psychic, the Plutonian Instruments making people more sexual, etc.

Saturnian Instruments – Chas Addams, John Agar, Louisa May Alcott, Cher Bono Allman, Robert Altman, Jean Anouilh, Fred Astaire, Joan Baez, Aubrey Beardsley, Rudolph Bing, Georges Bizet, Bernard Baruch, Dyan Cannon, Eddie Cantor, David Carradine, Johnny Carson, Catherine the Great of Russia, Edith Cavell, Carol Channing, Mark David Chapman, Maurice Chevalier, Julia Child, Winston Churchill, Pope Clement VII, Montgomery Clift, Ronald Colman, Sean Con-

nery, Jean-Batisse Corot, Linda Darnell, Doris Day, Dr. Tom
Dooley, Hugh Downs, Alexandre Dumas, Edward VII of
England, Federico Fellini, Henry Fonda, Francisco Franco,
Indira Gandhi, John Gavin, Ulysses S. Grant, Nathaniel
Hawthorne, Florence Henderson, Charlton Heston, Emperor
Hirohito of Japan, Anthony Hopkins, Harry Houdini, Jennifer
Jones, Jim Jones, Carl G. Jung, Edward M. Kennedy, Jack
Kerouac, Ken Kesey, Christopher Lee, Janet Leigh, Alan
Leo, Carole Lombard, Myrna Loy, Edouard Manet, Willie
Mays, Zubin Mehta, Maria Montessori, Bill Moyers, Iris
Murdoch, Ralph Nader, Jawaharlal Nehru, Willie Nelson,
Kim Novak, Eugene O'Neill, John J. O'Neill, General George
S. Patton, Czar Peter the Great of Russia, J. B. Priestley, Ira
Progoff, Robert Redford, Jerry Reed, Prince Zoorosh Ali Reza
of Iran, Jane Roberts, Jackie Robinson, Camille Saint-Saëns,
George Bernard Shaw, Percy Bysshe Shelley, Shirley Temple,
Margaret Thatcher, Martin Van Buren, Theodora Van Runkle,
Dennis Weaver, Simone Weil, Walt Whitman, Kaiser Wilhelm
II, Harold Wilson, Robert Anton Wilson, Emile Zola.

Uranian Instruments – Eddie Albert, Jr., Prince Andrew of
England, Anthony Armstrong-Jones, James Arness, John
Logie Baird, Martin Balsam, Honoré de Balzac, Ludwig van
Beethoven, Jacques Bergerac, Shelley Berman, Leonard Bern-
stein, Julian Bond, William Jennings Bryan, William F.
Buckley, Jr., Carol Burnett, John Calvin, Charles E. O. Carter,
Paul Foster Case, Johnny Cash, Edgar Cayce, Coco Channel,
James Coburn, Aleister Crowley, Adelle Davis, Angela Davis,
Edgar Degas, Cecil B. DeMille, Charles Dickens, Jeanne
Dixon, Kirk Douglas, Keir Dullea, Elizabeth II of England,
Ralph Waldo Emerson, Mia Farrow, Wilhelm Furtwängler,
Peggy Ann Garner, Charles de Gaulle, Llewellyn George, Vitas
Gerulaitas, Kahlil Gibran, Allen Ginsberg, Samuel Goldwyn,
Farley Granger, Rex Harrison, Franz Joseph Haydn, William
Randolph Hearst, Adolph Hitler, L. Ron Hubbard, Ben
Hunter, Peter Hurd, Andrew Jackson, Thomas Jefferson,
Ethel Kennedy, Rose Kennedy, Rudyard Kipling, Sandy
Koufax, Elisabeth Kübler-Ross, R. D. Laing, Sir Harry Lauder,
Anton van Leeuwenhoek, Charles Lindbergh, Julie London,
George Lucas, Clare Booth Luce, Charles Manson, Guglielmo
Marconi, Princess Margaret Rose of England, Eugene
McCarthy, Adolph Menjou, Amedeo Modigliani, Walter
Mondale, J. Pierpoint Morgan, Sr., Jack Parr, Jean Peters,

Franklin Delano Roosevelt, Charles Stuart II of England, Margaret Sullavan, Leon Trotsky, Gwen Verdon, Voltaire, Johnny Weissmuller, Peter Wolf, Jo Anne Worley.

Neptunian Instruments – Hank Aaron, Evangeline Adams, Konrad Adenauer, Herb Alpert, Eddie Arcaro, Lauren Bacall, Lucille Ball, Rona Barrett, Alan Bean, Philip Berrigan, David Bowie, Benjamin Britten, Robert Browning, Richard Burton, Steve Cauthen, Dick Cavett, Robert Conrad, Alice Cooper, Gary Cooper, Dino DeLaurentis, Faye Dunaway, Havelock Ellis, Geraldine Farrar, Nina Foch, Harrison Ford, Fulcanelli, Greta Garbo, Ava Gardner, Leif Garrett, George V of England, Alex Haley, Brett Harte, Jean Houston, Victor Hugo, Christopher Isherwood, Czar Ivan the Terrible of Russia, Burl Ives, Derek Jacobi, Johannes Kepler, Morgana King, David Kopay, Don Loper, Sophia Loren, Joseph Losey, Louis XIV of France, Louis XI of France, Don McLean, William McKinley, Edgar Dean Mitchell, Marilyn Monroe, Colleen Moore, Mary Tyler Moore, Roger Moore, Emperor Mutsuhito Meiji Tenno of Japan, Ricky Nelson, Eleanor Parker, Pope Paul VI, Luciano Pavarotti, Dory Previn, Marcel Proust, Raphael of Urbino, James Earl Ray, Della Reese, Richard II of England, Auguste Rodin, Rose Marie, Jerry Rubin, Jane Russell, Françoise Sagan, Jay Sebring, Jean Sibelius, Paul Simon, Sissy Spacek, Richard Speck, Robert Stack, Cat Stevens, Robert Louis Stevenson, Sally Struthers, James Taylor, Renata Tebaldi, Peter Ustinov, Maurice Utrillo, George Washington, Prince William of Wales.

Plutonian Instruments – Buzz Aldrin, Jack Anderson, Lucie Arnaz, Brigitte Bardot, Polly Bergen, Tycho Brahe, Werner von Braun, David Brinkley, Charles Bronson, Jerry Brown, Dave Brubeck, Edgar Rice Burroughs, Truman Capote, Prince Charles of England, Eldridge Cleaver, Gary Collins, Nicolas Copernicus, Bob Crane, Gabriele D'Annunzio, Rennie Davis, Albrecht Dürer, Adolph Eichmann, Elizabeth I of England, Keith Emerson, Bobbie Fischer, John Frankenheimer, David Frost, Art Garfunkel, Judy Garland, General Charles Gordon, Marjoe Gortner, Kathryn Grayson, Merv Griffin, Franz Hartmann, Herbert Hoover, Marilyn Horne, Peter Hurkos, Mick Jagger, Jean-Claude Killy, Henry Kissinger, T. E. Lawrence, Jerry Lewis, Abraham Lincoln, Stéphane Mallarmé, Jayne Mansfield, Steve McQueen, Robin Moore, Muhammad Ali, Alfred de Musset, Jack Nicholson, Clifford

Odets, Madalyn Murray O'Hair, Sir Laurence Olivier, Ryan O'Neal, Lee Harvey Oswald, Geraldine Page, Ram Dass, Christopher Reeve, Max Roach, John D. Rockefeller, Gene Roddenberry, Richard Rodgers, Ginger Rogers, Jimmy Rogers, Pete Rozelle, George Sand, Willie Shoemaker, Dinah Shore, Bobby Short, Phoebe Snow, Sharon Tate, John Travolta, Lana Turner, Liv Ullman, Al Unser, Arthur Wellesley (Duke of Wellington), Hank Williams, Jonathan Winters, Loretta Young.

Mixed Instruments: ● Saturn and Uranus – Ann-Margret, John Denver, Clark Gable, George VI of England, George Gershwin, Heinrich Himmler, John Lennon, Bob Mackie, James Monroe, Troy Perry, Maximilien Robespierre, Julie Sommars, Jon Voight, Ethel Waters, Charles Joseph Whitman. ● Saturn and Neptune – Jeff Bridges, Mary Cassatt, Howard Cosell, Benjamin Franklin, General Douglas MacArthur, General George Marshall, Jay Waverley North. ● Saturn and Pluto – Rollie Fingers, Johann Wolfgang von Goethe, James Madison, Karl Marx, Robert S. McNamara, Vance Packard, John Ruskin, Robert Shaw (of the Chorale), Mark Spitz, Andreas Vesalius, Orson Welles, Edgar Winter. ● Uranus and Neptune – Mary Baker Eddy, Pierre-Auguste Renoir, Pope Saint Pius X. ● Uranus and Pluto – Alexander Graham Bell, Annie Besant, Prince Naruhito of Japan, Nikola Tesla. ● Neptune and Pluto – Fattie Arbuckle, Joan Bennett, John Cage, Jean Cocteau, Isadora Duncan, Fernandel, Juliana of the Netherlands, Marcel Proust, Knute Rockne, Billy Rose, Adlai Stevenson, Walter Winchell. ● Saturn, Neptune and Pluto – Lon Chaney, Sr., Hedy Lamarr.

The Adepts (An Absence of One Element or Quality for the Planets and the Ascendant)

Fire Adepts (neither the Ascendant nor any planet in Fire Signs) are experts in matters having to do with Aries, Leo, Sagittarius, the 1st House, the 5th House and the 9th House in terms of helping others with concerns of these life areas. However, their expertise cannot be applied to their own lives until the Adept is brought into consciousness within themselves.

Fire Adepts – Faith Baldwin, John Barrymore, Sr., Richard Basehart, Jack Benny, Hugo Black, Margaret Bourke-White,

Lord Byron, Dyan Cannon, Diahann Carroll, Charles E. O. Carter, Eldridge Cleaver, Geraldine Farrar, Wilhelm Furtwängler, Zsa Zsa Gabor, Leif Garrett, George Frederick Handel, William Henry Harrison, Rutherford B. Hayes, J. Edgar Hoover, Hubert H. Humphrey, Peter Hurkos, John Keats, Johannes Kepler, William Lily, Dolly Madison, Meher Baba, Adolph Menjou, Merle Oberon, Aristotle Onassis, Louis Pasteur, Pope Paul VI, Pope Pius XI, Vincent Price, J. B. Priestley, Giancomo Puccini, Rembrandt van Rijn, Roy Rogers, Franklin Delano Roosevelt, Rosalind Russell, Babe Ruth, Jean Paul Sartre, Brooke Shields, Upton Sinclair, Donald Sutherland, Gus Trikonis, Rudolph Valentino, Earl Warren.

Earth Adepts (neither the Ascendant nor any planet in Earth Signs) are experts in matters having to do with Taurus, Virgo, Capricorn, the 2nd House, the 6th House and the 10th House in terms of helping others with concerns of these life areas. However, their expertise cannot be applied to their own lives until the Adept is brought into consciousness.

Earth Adepts – Abdul-Bahá, Kareem Abdul-Jabbar, Harry Belafonte, Frank Borman, Helen Gurley Brown, Andrew Carnegie, Mary Cassatt, Roger Chaffee, Georges Clemenceau, Grover Cleveland, Jackie Coogan, Joan Crawford, Jack Dempsey, Phyllis Diller, Joe DiMaggio, Sandy Duncan, Chris Evert, Farrah Fawcett, Sally Field, Zelda Fitzgerald, Peggy Fleming, Larry Flynt, Art Garfunkel, Judy Garland, George VI of England, Jackie Gleason, Francisco de Goya, Kathryn Grayson, Billy Graham, Hetty Green, Virgil Grissom, Susan Hayward, Jimi Hendrix, Heinrich Himmler, Paul Hindemith, Lena Horne, Ken Howard, Jennifer Jones, Marc Edmund Jones, Ethel Kennedy, Elisabeth Kübler-Ross, Hedy Lamarr, Christopher Lee, Gypsy Rose Lee, Janet Leigh, Martin Luther, Norman Mailer, Katherine Mansfield, Dick Martin, Bette Midler, Marilyn Monroe, Colleen Moore, Audie Murphy, Vaslav Nijinsky, Eugene O'Neill, Nicolò Paganini, Geraldine Page, Eleanor Parker, Pier Paolo Pasolini, Mary Pickford, Franklin Pierce, Raphael of Urbino, James Earl Ray, Gioacchino Antonio Rossini, Dane Rudhyar, Martin Scorsese, O. J. Simpson, Cat Stevens, Robert Louis Stevenson, Algernon Swinburne, Alfred Lord Tennyson, Arthur Treacher, Mark Twain, Sir Anthony Van Dyck, Theodora Van Runkle, Lawrence Welk, Tennessee Williams, Emile Zola.

Air Adepts (neither the Ascendant nor any planet in Air Signs) are experts in matters having to do with Gemini, Libra, Aquarius, the 3rd House, the 7th House and the 11th House in terms of helping others with concerns of these life areas. However, their expertise cannot be applied to their own lives until the Adept is made conscious within them.

Air Adepts – Czar Alexander II of Russia, Prince Andrew of England, Sri Aurobindo, Pierre Charles Baudelaire, Aubrey Beardsley, Warren Beatty, Ray Bradbury, Marlon Brando, Emily Brontë, Anita Bryant, William F. Buckley, Jr., Bernard Buffet, Glen Campbell, Billy Carter, Steve Cauthen, Edgar Cayce, Cheiro, Mike Connors, Francis Ford Coppola, Bob Crane, Dino DeLaurentis, Faye Dunaway, David Frost, Llewellyn George, Vincent van Gogh, Pancho Gonzales, Farley Granger, Ulysses S. Grant, Merv Griffin, Alex Haley, Mata Hari, Dustin Hoffman, Pope John XXIII, Jim Jones, Helen Keller, Ethel Kennedy, Robert F. Kennedy, Bruce Lee, Anton van Leeuwenhoek, Liberace, Gina Lollobrigida, Guy de Maupassant, Willie Mays, Zubin Mehta, Patrice Munsel, Czar Nicholas II of Russia, Jack Nicholson, Florence Nightingale, Ram Dass, Dan Rather, Robert Redford, Jerry Reed, Prince Zoorosh Ali Reza of Iran, Gene Roddenberry, Will Rogers, Sr., Edmond Rostand, Johann Christoph Friedrich von Schiller, David Shire, Jean Sibelius, Upton Sinclair, Baruch Spinoza, Joseph Stalin, Leo Tolstoy, Lily Tomlin, Lee Trevino, Peter Ustinov, Jack Valenti, Raquel Welch, Edward White, Jr., Esther Williams.

Water Adepts (neither the Ascendant nor any planet in Water Signs) are experts in matters having to do with Cancer, Scorpio, Pisces, the 4th House, the 8th House and the 12th House in terms of helping others with concerns of these life areas. However, their expertise cannot be applied to their own lives until the Adepts are brought into consciousness within themselves.

Water Adepts – Greg Allman, Ann-Margret, Joan Baez, Aubrey Beardsley, Ludwig van Beethoven, John Belushi, Rudolph Bing, Tycho Brahe, Berthold Brecht, Edgar Rice Burroughs, Lewis Carroll, Maurice Chevalier, Gary Cooper, Xavier Cugat, Angela Davis, Marlene Dietrich, Faye Dunaway, Joe Frazier, Frederick the Great, Charles de Gaulle, George V of England, Kahlil Gibran, Samuel Goldwyn, Marjoe Gortner, Edvard Grieg, Franz Joseph Haydn, O. Henry, Emperor

Hirohito of Japan, Adolph Hitler, Herbert Hoover, Mick Jagger, Henry J. Kaiser, Jean-Claude Killy, Evel Knievel, Fernand Leger, Maurice Maeterlinck, Edouard Manet, General George Marshall, Muhammad Ali, Louis Pasteur, Drew Pearson, Valerie Perrine, Jonathan Swift, Rabindranath Tagore, Maurice Utrillo, Ritchie Valens, Swami Vivekananda, Sulamith Wülfing, William Butler Yeats.

Cardinal Adepts (neither the Ascendant nor any planet in Cardinal Signs) are experts in matters having to do with Aries, Cancer, Libra, Capricorn, the 1st House, the 4th House, the 7th House and the 10th House in terms of helping others with concerns of these life areas. However, their expertise cannot be applied to their own lives until the Adept is made conscious within themselves.

Cardinal Adepts – Albert of England (Prince Consort), Bob Dylan, John Wayne Gacey, Bruno Hauptmann, Victor Hugo, Mick Jagger, Bruce Lee, Anton van Leeuwenhoek, Henry Wadsworth Longfellow, Pat O'Brien, James Knox Polk, Brooke Shields, Baruch Spinoza, Rudolph Steiner, Ritchie Valens.

Fixed Adepts (neither the Ascendant nor any planet in Fixed Signs) are experts in matters to do with Taurus, Leo, Scorpio, Aquarius, the 2nd House, the 5th House, the 8th House and the 11th House on terms of helping others with concerns of these life areas. However, their expertise cannot be applied to their own lives until the Adept is brought into consciousness within themselves.

Fixed Adepts – Grand Duchess Anastasia of Russia, Elizabeth Barrett Browning, Sean Connery, Gareth Knight.

Mutable Adepts (neither the Ascendant nor any planet in Mutable Signs) are experts in matters having to do with Gemini, Virgo, Sagittarius, Pisces, the 3rd House, the 6th House, the 9th House and the 12th House in terms of helping others with concerns of these life areas. However, their expertise cannot be applied to their own lives until the Adept is brought into consciousness within themselves.

Mutable Adepts – Guy Ballard, Thor Heyerdahl, Yehudi Menuhin, Richard III of England, Bertrand Russell, Camille Saint-Saëns, Emperor Tiberius of Rome, Arturo Toscanini.

The Mutual Reception Aliens have the same abilities as the type of Alien which the mutual reception of two planetary

factors (including the Sun and Moon) create in them: **Power,
Vessel** or **Instrument.** The difference between the 'natural'
Aliens and the mutual reception Aliens seems to be that the
latter can allow their inherent talents and abilities lie qui-
escent while the 'natural' Alien internal constructs push from
within for awakening.

Mutual Reception Uranian Powers – Princess Caroline of
Marjoe Gortner, Carol Landis, John C. Lilly, Guy Madison,
Gary Middlecoff, Henry Miller, J. D. Salinger, Austin O.
Spare, Robert Stack, Edgar Winter, Jane Wyman.

Mutual reception Uranian Powers – Princess Caroline of
Monaco, Mia Farrow, Farrah Fawcett, Fulcanelli, Peggy Ann
Garner, Janis Joplin, Edward M. Kennedy, Charles Lamb,
Fernand Leger, Amy Lowell, Gertrude Stein, Sharon Tate,
François Truffaut.

Mutual Reception Neptunian Powers – Robert Altman,
Harry Belafonte, Jack Benny, Shelley Berman, Anthony
Burgess, Taylor Caldwell, Herb Elliot, Yuri Gagarin, Jackie
Gleason, Charles Goren, Peter Graves, Joan Hackett, Patty
Hearst, Jennifer Jones, Jack Kerouac, Harold MacMillan,
Marcello Mastroianni, Steve McQueen, Sean O'Faolain, Pier
Paolo Pasolini, Linus Pauling, Sam Peckinpah, Sidney Poitier,
James Earl Ray, Cliff Robertson, Walter Schirra, Peter Sellers,
Elizabeth Taylor, Earl Warren, Peter Wolf.

Mutual Reception Plutonian Powers – David Ben-Gurion,
Constance Bennett, Alexander Borodin, Cyd Charisse, Prince
Charles of England, Jimmy Connors, Nicholas Culpepper,
John Dewey, Keith Emerson, Rollie Fingers, Larry Flynt, Paul
Joseph Goebbels, Goldie Hawn, Bruce Jenner, Billie Jean
King, André Malraux, Pelé, Ezra Pound, Helen Reddy, F.
Israel Regardie, Roy Rogers, Martin Scorsese, Grace Slick,
Phoebe Snow, John Philip Sousa, Robert Louis Stevenson,
Henry Winkler, Harris Yulin.

Mutual Reception Saturnian-Uranian Powers – Howard
Hughes, W. Somerset Maugham.

Mutual Reception Saturnian-Neptunian Powers – Desi
Arnaz, Sr., George Lincoln Rockwell.

Mutual Reception Saturnian-Plutonian Powers – Larry
Csonka, Sally Field, Diane von Furstenberg, Alan Watts.

Mutual Reception Uranian-Neptunian Powers – Pierre-
Auguste Renoir.

Mutual Reception Uranian-Plutonian **Powers** – Admiral Richard E. Byrd.

Mutual Reception Neptunian-Plutonian **Powers**–Vincenzo Bellini, Fanny Brice, Galilei Galileo, Victor Hugo.

Mutual Reception Saturnian **Vessels** – Cher Bono Allman, Richard Basehart, Hugo Black, Napoleon Buonaparte, Mia Farrow, Federico Fellini, Elbert Hubbard, Carol Landis, Ernst von Lubitsch, George Meredith, General George S. Patton, Gian-Franco Zeffirelli.

Mutual Reception Uranian **Vessels**– David Cassidy, Prince Charles Edward Stuart of England, Jimmy Connors, John Galsworthy, Bruce Jenner, Linda Lovelace, Piet Mondrian, Muhammad Ali, François Truffaut, H. G. Wells.

Mutual Reception Neptunian **Vessels** – Desi Arnaz, Jr., Lew Ayres, Margaret Bourke-White, Allesandro di Cagliostro, David Cassidy, Claudette Colbert, Ian Fleming, Johann Wolfgang von Goethe, Christopher Isherwood, Howard Lindsay, Jeanette MacDonald, Marcello Mastroianni, Vincent Price, Erick Maria Remarque, Richard Rodgers, Dane Rudhyar, Antoine de Saint-Exupéry.

Mutual Reception Plutonian **Vessels**– Hank Aaron, Warren Beatty, Dave Brubeck, Truman Capote, Art Carney, Billy Carter, Jimmy Carter, Johnny Cash, Otis Chandler, Francis Ford Coppola, Norman Cousins, Miles Davis, James Dean, Farouk of Egypt, John Frankenheimer, David Frost, David Garroway, Alex Haley, Lena Horne, Mario Lanza, John Mitchell, Michael J. Pollard, Ram Dass, James Earl Ray, Alain Resnais, Willie Shoemaker, Tom Smothers, Risë Stevens, Elizabeth Taylor, Ingrid Thulin, Jack Valenti.

Mutual Reception Saturnian-Plutonian **Vessels** – Zsa Zsa Gabor, Farley Granger, Dennis Weaver.

Mutual Reception Uranian-Neptunian **Vessels** – Paul Cézanne, Georges Clemenceau.

Mutual Reception Neptunian-Plutonian **Vessels** – Hector Berlioz.

Mutual Reception Saturnian **Instruments** – Larry Csonka, John C. Lilly.

Mutual Reception Uranian **Instruments** – David Lloyd George, Piet Mondrian.

Mutual Reception Neptunian **Instruments** – Desi Arnaz, Jr., Leigh Taylor-Young.

Mutual Reception Plutonian **Instruments**– Edward Asner,

Stephen Collins Foster, Marc Edmund Jones, F. Israel Regardie.

Mutual Reception Saturnian-Uranian Instruments – Dyan Cannon.

Mutual Reception Saturnian-Plutonian Instruments – Dennis Weaver.

Mutual Reception Neptunian-Plutonian Instruments – Abraham Lincoln.

18.

People, Famous and Infamous, Without 'Alien' Patterns

Cannonball Adderly, Alfred Adler, Spiro Agnew, Prince Akihito of Japan, Prince Albert Victor of England, Prince Albert of Monaco, Alan Alda, Czarevitch Alexis of Russia, Steve Allen, Hans Christian Anderson, Julie Andrews, Arthur Ashe, Robert Assagioli, Mary Astor, John James Audubon, Wilhelm Backhaus, Jim Backus, F. Lee Bailey, Pearl Bailey, Anne Baxter, Wallace Beery, Candice Bergen, Ingrid Bergman, Daniel Berrigan, Otto von Bismarck, Dirk Bogarde, Debbie Boone, Pat Boone, Johannes Brahms, Willy Brandt, Rossano Brazzi, Beau Bridges, Art Buchwald, Albert Camus, Al Capone, Barbara Cartland, George Washington Carver, Shaun Cassidy, Carlos Castaneda, Richard Chamberlain, Wilt Chamberlain, Joe Chambers, Ilka Chase, Charlie Chaplin, Hope Cooke, Arnold Dean Corll, Gustave Courbet, Buster Crabbe, Stephen Crane, Salvador Dali, John Dean, Claude Debussy, Alain Delon, Benjamin Disraeli, Princess Diana of England, Emily Dickinson, The Dionne Quintuplets, Christian Dior, Fedor Dostoyevski, Lord Alfred Douglas, Lesley-Anne Down, Theodore Dreiser, Clint Eastwood, Edward VIII of England (Duke of Windsor), George Eliot, Herb Elliot, Carl Erskine, Douglas Fairbanks, Jr., William Falkner, Jose Feliciano, Edna Ferber, Enrico Fermi, F. Scott Fitzgerald, Peter Finch, Camille Flammarion, Sir Alexander Fleming, Jane Fonda, Peter Fonda, Arthur Ford, Betty Ford, Glenn Ford, Henry Ford, Tony Franciosa, Aretha Franklin, Robert Fulton, Mahatma Gandhi, James A. Garfield, Paul Gauguin, Uri Geller, André Gide, John H. Glenn, Jr., Robert Goulet, Charles Gounod, Juliette Greco, Georges Gurdjieff, Arlo Guthrie, Gene Hackman, Merle Haggard, Manly Palmer Hall, Thomas Hardy, Benjamin Harrison, Helen Hayes, Rita

Hayworth, Hugh Hefner, Max Heindel, Ernest Hemingway, Henry II of England, Henry VIII of England, Audrey Hepburn, Katherine Hepburn, James Hilton, John Warnock Hinckley, Jr., Alfred Hitchcock, Hal Holbrook, Celeste Holm, Miriam Hopkins, Hussein of Jordan, Thomas Henry Huxley, Washington Irving, Elton John, Pope John Paul I, Andrew Johnson, Ladybird Johnson, Lyndon B. Johnson, Samuel Johnson, Tom Jones, Christine Jorgenson, James Joyce, Immanuel Kant, Diane Keaton, Grace Kelly, John Fitzgerald Kennedy, Martin Luther King, Jr., Arthur Koestler, Jiddu Krishnamurti, Kris Kristofferson, Edouard Lalo, Burt Lancaster, Eva LeGallienne, Leonardo da Vinci, Nathan Leopold, John L. Jewis, Joshua Logan, Louis XVI of France Michael Love ('Beach Boys'), Bela Lugosi, Paul Lynde, Nicolo Machiavelli, Gustave Mahler, Moses ben Maimon, Henry Mancini, Joseph Mankiewicz, Thomas Mann, Jean Marais, Marie Antoinette of France, Groucho Marx, Mary of England, Bob Mathias, André Maurois, Rollo May, Joseph R. McCarthy, Michael McClure, Roddy McDowell, Felix Mendelssohn, Melina Mercouri, Jean-François Millet, Jeanne Moreau, Jim Morrison, Gurudev Muktananda, Graham Nash, Patricia Neal, Paul Newman, Sir Isaac Newton, Beverly Nichols, Jack Nicklaus, Friedrich Nietzsche, Birgit Nilssen, Christina Onassis, Jacqueline Kennedy Onassis, Carl Orff, Gregory Peck, George Peppard, Pablo Picasso, Auguste Piccard, Sylvia Plath, Tyrone Power, Leontyne Price, Freddie Prinz, Giacomo Puccini, Ernie Pyle, Rainier III of Monaco, Maurice Ravel, Johnny Ray, Steve Reeves, Ottorino Respighi, Burt Reynolds, Carroll Righter, Arthur Rimbaud, Edward G. Robinson, Kenny Rogers, General Erwin Rommel, Theodore Roosevelt, Philip Roth, Jill St John, Carl Sandburg, George Santayana, William Saroyan, Arthur Schlesinger, Jr., Max Schmeling, Franz Schubert, Robert Schumann, David R. Scott, George C. Scott, Rod Serling, Georges Seurat, Frank Sinatra, Sirhan Sirhan, Walter Slezak, Tom Snyder, Albert Speer, Jess Stearn, Gloria Steinem, Robert Taft, Michael Tilson Thomas, Rip Torn, Henri Toulouse-Lautrec, Giuseppe Verdei, Jules Verne, Victoria of England, Gore Vidal, Richard Wagner, Dennis Wheatley, John Greenleaf Whittier, Richard Widmark, Oscar Wilde, Gene Wilder, Kaiser Wilhelm II of Germany, Woodrow Wilson, Jane Withers, Frank Lloyd Wright, Glenn Yarbrough, Paramahansa Yogananda.

19.

Use of the I Ching or Book of Changes with the Inner Guide Meditation

The *I Ching* is recommended as an excellent tool to use to help get through the Magic Mirror Effect that occurs in meditation. It is the best 'ego check' I have found to date. When you feel that the answer you have received in meditation or the action that has been recommended goes too much along with your desires or ego wishes (and doubt occurs), ask the *I Ching*'s advice on acting or not acting on the answer or request for action. The *coin method* for use with the *I Ching* is given below.

The recommended *I Ching* book is the Wilhelm/Baynes edition published by Princeton University Press. The coin method given here is from C. G. Jung's *Man and His Symbols*. According to the latter, when using Western coins:

$$\text{Heads} = 3$$
$$\text{Tails} = 2$$

Cast *three* coins *six* times listing the total of each throw on paper. Have your question in mind when doing this. Build the column of totals *from bottom to top* (like building a house). For example:

7 = 1 head, 2 tails (last throw)
8 = 2 heads, 1 tail (5th throw)
6 = 3 tails (4th throw)
7 = 1 head, 2 tails (3rd throw)
9 = 3 heads (2nd throw)
7 = 1 head, 2 tails (1st throw)

The *odd* numbers are represented by a straight unbroken line and the *even* numbers by a broken line. Next to each number, place its corresponding line. Again, work from bottom to top:

'Tree of Life' Sphere *Yesod* from the D.O.M.E. Meditation Cards by Sheila W. Ross.

```
↑ 7 ——————
  8 ——   ——
  6 ——   ——
  7 ——————
  9 ——————
  7 ——————
```

The pattern the six lines form is called a *hexagram*, and is composed of a top and a bottom *trigram*, or group of three lines.

Now turn to the chart of hexagrams at the back of the *I Ching* book. Notice that the first three lines in our sample hexagram are *straight, straight, straight* (reading from the bottom up). These bottom three lines are called the *lower trigram*. Find the corresponding *straight, straight, straight* lines on the hexagram chart in the column marked 'Lower Trigram' on the left. You will find this pattern of lines called *Ch'ien*. Then notice the top three lines of the sample hexagram. They are *broken, broken, straight*. The top three lines are called the 'Upper trigram'. Find the corresponding upper trigram on the hexagram chart across the top of the page, and you will find it named *Ken*. Now the box where *Ch'ien* and *Ken* come together is the square numbered 26. This is the number of the *first hexagram* of your answer.

Now the lines that total 6 and 9 always *change* into their opposites. 6, which starts out broken becomes a straight line, and 9 which starts out as a straight line becomes a broken line. (7's and 8's always remain the same, not changing into their opposites.) The sample now looks like this:

```
7 ——————        ——————
8 ——   ——        ——   ——
6 ——   ——        ——————
7 ——————        ——————
9 ——————        ——   ——
7 ——————        ——————
```

Note that in the second hexagram the lines corresponding to the 9 and the 6 are now opposite what they were in the first hexagram. Looking up the second pair of trigrams in the key in the back of the *I Ching* identifies them as *Li* over *Li* or hexagram 30. Place this number at the bottom of the second hexagram. Now you are ready to read the *I Ching's* answer to your question.

Turn to hexagram 26 in *Book I* of the *Text* and begin reading through 'The Judgement' and 'The Image' up to where it says 'The Lines'. 'The Lines' refer to the *changing* lines in the *first* hexagram (6's and 9's, not 7's and 8's). Since, in our sample hexagram 26, the first or bottom line is not a 6 or a 9, we go to the line called '9 in the 2nd place'. This is the first *sequential change* (relative to the question) that operates against the *background* of 'The Judgement' and 'The Image' of hexagram 26. Then skip to the 4th place in the hexagram (the *next* changing line) and read the paragraph which begins '6 in the 4th place means'.

That is all there is to read in hexagram 26. (First read up to 'The Lines' in *any first hexagram*, and then read only the *changing* lines in that hexagram). 'The Judgement' and 'The Image' give you the *background* of the situation being asked about, and the changing 'Lines' give the sequential changes that will happen against that background. To complete the reading turn to the 2nd hexagram, *30*, and read only 'The Judgement' and 'The Image'. *Never read any lines in a 2nd Hexagram.* The 2nd hexagram indicates the *end result* of the question and never has 'Lines' to read.

There is one kind of hexagram to be considered. It occurs when all the totals turn out to be 7's and 8's. This is a *Fated* hexagram and never has 'Lines' to read. It is a situation already *set* in time and space.

When wording your questions, it is best to avoid questions beginning with 'Should . . .' *The Book of Changes* is set up to show sequential action in time. The clearest answers come as the result of *two separate questions* regarding any one situation: 'If I *do* such and such what will be the end result?' and if I *don't do* such and such what will be the end result?' This presents the two possible time flows. A simple 'What's happening?' will serve to clarify confusing life situations.

Remember, the *I Ching* or *Book of Changes* always is speaking to the 'superior' or *conscious* person.

Some suggestions for interpreting the *I Ching*'s words:

Superior = Conscious
Inferior = Unconscious
Man = Masculine, creative principle in a man or a woman
Woman = Feminine, receptive principle in a man or a woman

Great Man = The Inner Guide
King or Prince = the Self or Centre in a man or a woman

20.

Astrological Symbols and Patterns

Symbols of the Planets		Other Astrological Symbols		Astrological Patterns
Sun	☉	Moon's True North Node ☊		T-CROSS formed by 2 planets
Moon	☽	Moon's True South Node ☋		in opposition and a 3rd planet
Mercury	☿	Part of Fortune ⊗		squaring both
Venus	♀	Retrograde ℞		GRAND SQUARE formed by 4
Mars	♂	Stationary s		planets squaring each other
Jupiter	♃	Direct ᴅ		around the horoscope (two op-
Saturn	♄	Conjunction (0°) ☌		positions squaring each other)
Uranus	♅	Sextile (60°) ✶		GRAND TRINE formed by 3
Neptune	♆	Quintile (72°) ꝙ		planets each 120° from
Pluto	♇	Square (90°) ☐		each other
Earth	⊕	Trine (120°) △		YOD CROSS formed by 2
		Quincunx (150°) ⊼		sextiles planets each 150° from
		Opposition (180°) ☍		a 3rd (also called 'The Finger
		Parallel of Declination (0°) ℗		of God')

21.
Symbols and Rulerships of the 12 Signs of the Zodiac

Aries ♈ Cardinal Fire, Ruler Mars ♂

Taurus ♉ Fixed Earth, Ruler Venus ♀

Gemini ♊ Mutable Air, Ruler Mercury ☿

Cancer ♋ Cardinal Water, Ruler Moon ☽

Leo ♌ Fixed Fire, Ruler Sun ☉

Virgo ♍ Mutable Earth, Ruler Mercury ☿

Libra ♎ Cardinal Air, Ruler Venus ♀

Scorpio ♏ Fixed Water, Ruler Pluto ♇

Sagittarius ♐ Mutable Fire, Ruler Jupiter ♃

Capricorn ♑ Cardinal Earth, Ruler Saturn ♄

Aquarius ♒ Fixed Air, Ruler Uranus ♅

Pisces ♓ Mutable Water, Ruler Neptune ♆

Woodcut of 'The Northern Hemisphere of the Celestial Globe' by Albrecht Dürer (c.1515).

22.

Transiting Positions of Pluto, Neptune, Uranus and Saturn from 1-1-65

DECANS OF ANY SIGN:
1st – 0°01' to 10°00'
2nd – 10°01' to 20°00'
3rd – 20°01' to 30°00'

PLUTO – The Last Judgement

2nd Decan Virgo ♍	1-1-65 to 11-3-66, 2-12-67 to 9-1-67
3rd Decan Virgo	11-3-66 to 2-12-67, 9-1-67 to 10-5-71, 4-17-72 to 7-30-72
1st Decan Libra ♎	10-5-71 to 4-17-72, 7-30-72 to 10-25-75, 4-12-76 to 8-21-76
2nd Decan Libra	10-25-75 to 4-12-76, 8-21-76 to 11-3-79, 4-24-80 to 8-29-80
3rd Decan Libra	11-3-79 to 4-24-80, 8-29-80 to 11-5-83, 5-18-84 to 8-27-84
1st Decan Scorpio ♏	11-5-83 to 5-18-84, 8-27-84 to 11-4-87

NEPTUNE – The Hanged Man

2nd Decan Scorpio ♏	1-1-65 to 11-19-65, 6-12-66 to 9-18-66
3rd Decan Scorpio	11-19-65 to 6-12-66, 9-18-66 to 1-5-70, 5-3-70 to 11-6-70

1st Decan Sagittarius ♐	1-5-70 to 5-3-70, 11-6-70 to 12-19-74, 6-17-75 to 10-22-75
2nd Decan Sagittarius	12-19-74 to 6-17-75, 10-22-75 to 2-8-79, 5-6-79 to 12-7-79, 8-13-80 to 9-20-80
3rd Decan Sagittarius	2-8-79 to 5-6-79, 12-7-79 to 8-13-80, 9-20-80 to 1-18-84, 6-22-84 to 11-21-84
1st Decan Capricorn ♑	1-18-84 to 6-22-84, 11-21-84 to 3-15-88

URANUS – The Fool

2nd Decan Virgo ♍	1-1-65 to 9-12-66
3rd Decan Virgo	9-12-66 to 9-28-68, 5-21-69 to 6-24-69
1st Decan Libra ♎	9-28-68 to 5-21-69, 6-24-69 to 10-15-70, 5-12-71 to 7-23-71
2nd Decan Libra	10-15-70 to 5-12-71, 7-23-71 to 11-1-72, 5-6-73 to 8-15-73
3rd Decan Libra	11-1-72 to 5-6-73, 8-15-73 to 11-21-74, 5-1-75 to 9-8-75
1st Decan Scorpio	11-21-74 to 5-1-75, 9-8-75 to 12-12-76, 4-24-77 to 9-30-77
2nd Decan Scorpio	12-12-76 to 4-24-77, 9-30-77 to 1-7-79, 4-15-79 to 10-23-79
3rd Decan Scorpio ♏	1-7-79 to 4-15-79, 10-23-79 to 2-17-81, 3-20-81 to 11-16-81
1st Decan Sagittarius ♐	2-17-81 to 3-20-81, 11-16-81 to 12-12-83, 7-15-84 to 9-20-84
2nd Decan Sagittarius	12-12-83 to 7-15-84, 9-20-84 to 1-9-86, 6-20-86 to 10-30-86
3rd Decan Sagittarius	1-9-86 to 6-20-86, 10-30-86 to 2-14-88

SATURN – The World

1st Decan Pisces ♓	1-1-65 to 3-18-65
2nd Decan Pisces	3-18-65 to 3-11-66
3rd Decan Pisces	3-11-66 to 3-3-67
1st Decan Aries ♈	3-3-67 to 5-30-67, 9-20-67 to 2-20-68
2nd Decan Aries	5-30-67 to 9-20-67, 2-20-68 to 5-13-68, 11-12-68 to 1-28-69
3rd Decan Aries	5-13-68 to 11-12-68, 1-28-69 to 4-29-69
1st Decan Taurus ♉	4-29-69 to 4-16-70
2nd Decan Taurus	4-16-70 to 7-10-70, 11-1-70 to 3-29-71
3rd Decan Taurus	7-10-70 to 11-1-70, 3-29-71 to 6-18-71, 1-10-72 to 2-21-72
1st Decan Gemini ♊	6-18-71 to 1-10-72, 2-21-72 to 5-31-72
2nd Decan Gemini	5-31-72 to 9-6-72, 10-28-72 to 5-13-73
3rd Decan Gemini	9-6-72 to 10-28-72, 5-13-73 to 8-1-73, 1-7-74 to 4-18-74
1st Decan Cancer ♋	8-1-73 to 1-7-74, 4-18-74 to 7-13-74
2nd Decan Cancer ♋	7-13-74 to 6-26-75
3rd Decan Cancer	6-26-75 to 9-17-75, 1-14-76 to 6-5-76
1st Decan Leo ♌	9-17-75 to 1-14-76, 6-5-76 to 8-25-76, 4-4-77 to 4-17-77
2nd Decan Leo	8-25-76 to 4-4-77, 4-17-77 to 8-10-77
3rd Decan Leo	8-10-77 to 11-16-77, 1-5-78 to 7-26-78

1st Decan Virgo ♍	11-16-77 to 1-5-78, 7-26-78 to 10-17-78, 3-8-79 to 7-8-79
2nd Decan Virgo	10-17-78 to 3-8-79, 7-8-79 to 10-2-79
3rd Decan Virgo	10-2-79 to 9-21-80
1st Decan Libra ♎	9-21-80 to 9-12-81
2nd Decan Libra	9-12-81 to 12-10-81, 3-25-82 to 9-4-82
3rd Decan Libra	12-10-81 to 3-25-82, 9-4-82 to 11-29-82, 5-6-83 to 8-24-83
1st Decan Scorpio ♏	11-29-82 to 5-6-83, 8-24-83 to 11-23-83, 6-23-84 to 8-1-84
2nd Decan Scorpio	11-23-83 to 6-23-84, 8-1-84 to 11-19-84
3rd Decan Scorpio	11-19-84 to 11-17-85
1st Decan Sagittarius ♐	11-17-85 to 11-15-86
2nd Decan Sagittarius	11-15-86 to 2-21-87, 5-8-87 to 11-14-87
3rd Decan Sagittarius	2-21-87 to 5-8-87, 11-14-87 to 2-13-88

Recommended Reading

*Those books and materials giving further information on tarot and the archetypes.

Bach, Richard. *Illusions.* Delacorte Press, 1977.

Bardon, Franz. *Initiation into Hermetics.* Osiris-Verlag, 1962.

Benner, J.S. *The Impersonal Life.* Willing, 1963.

Bentov, Itzhak. *Stalking the Wild Pendulum: On the Mechanics of Consciousness.* E. P. Dutton, 1977, paper.

Brennan, J. M. *Astral Doorways.* Weiser, 1971. *Experimental Magic.* Weiser, 1972. *Five Keys to Past Lives.* Weiser, 1971, paper.

Brunton, Paul. *A Search in Secret Egypt.* Weiser, 1970, paper.

Bullfinch's *Greek Mythology.* Many editions available.

Butler, W. E. *How to Develop Clairvoyance.* Weiser, 1968, paper. *How to Read the Aura.* Weiser, 1971, paper.

Carroll, Lewis. *Alice in Wonderland* and *Alice Through the Looking Glass.* Many editions available. (Aquarian Age stuff.)

Case, Paul Foster. *The Tarot: A Key to the Wisdom of the Ages.* Macoy, 1947.
The Book of Tokens: Tarot Meditations. Builders of the Adytum, 1968.

Cavendish, Richard. *The Black Arts.* Putnam, 1967, paper. (Poor title. Not so black. Good survey of the metaphysical field.)

Cirlot, J. E. *A Dictionary of Symbols. Philosophic Library, 1972.

Drury, Neville. Don Juan, Mescalito and Modern Magic: The Mythology of Inner Space. Routledge and Kegan Paul, 1978 paper.

Edinger, Edward F. *Ego and Archetype. Penguin, 1973, paper.

Fortune, Dion. The Cosmic Doctrine. Weiser, 1978, paper.
The Esoteric Philosophy of Love and Marriage. Weiser, 1978, paper.
*The Mystical Qabalah. Weiser, 1974.
Through the Gates of Death. Weiser, 1978, paper.

Golas, Thaddeus. The Lazy Man's Guide to Enlightenment. Seed Center, 1972, paper.

Grant, Joan. Winged Pharaoh. Berkly, 1958, paper. (All her books on 'far memory' are excellent, e.g. The Eyes of Horus, Lord of the Horizon, Life as Carola.)

Haich, Elizabeth. Initiation. Seed Center, 1974, paper.

Harding, M. Esther. *Woman's Mysteries, Ancient and Modern. Princeton University Press, 1977, paper.

Harner, Michael. The Way of the Shaman. Harper & Row, 1980.

Jung, Carl G. *Man and His Symbols. Doubleday, 1964, paper.
Memories, Dreams, Reflections. Vintage, 1965, paper.

Knight, Gareth. *Experience of the Inner Worlds. Helios, 1975.
A History of White Magic. Weiser, 1978, paper.
Occult Exercises and Practices. Weiser, 1969, paper.
*Practical Guide to Qabalistic Symbolism. Weiser, 1978.

Krishna, Gopi. The Awakening of Kundalini. E. P. Dutton, 1975, paper.
Kundalini, the Evolutionary Energy in Man. Shambhala, 1973, paper.

Kübler-Ross, Elisabeth. Death: The Final Stage of Growth. Prentice-Hall, 1975, paper.

Lao Tzu. Tao Te Ching. Many translations available. (Witter Bynner's is excellent: Capricorn, 1962, paper.)

Larsen, Stephen. *The Shaman's Doorway: Opening the Mythic Imagination to Contemporary Consciousness. Harper, 1976, paper.

Laurence, Theodor. *The Sexual Key to the Tarot. Citadel, 1971, paper.

Le Guin, Ursula K. The Earthsea Trilogy. (The Wizard of Earthsea. Bantam, 1968, paper. The Tombs of Atuan. Bantam, 1971, paper. The Farthest Shore. Bantam, 1972, paper.)

Lindsay, David. A Voyage to Arcturus. Ballantine, 1963, paper.

Monroe, Robert A. Journeys Out of the Body. Anchor, 1973, paper.

Moody, Raymond A., Jr. Life After Life. Bantam, 1975, paper.

Regardie, Israel. The Tree of Life. Weiser, 1969, paper.

Rendel, Peter. Introduction to the Chakras. Weiser, 1976, paper.

Richardson, Alan. An Introduction to the Mystical Qabalah. Weiser, 1974, paper.

Sanella, Lee. Kundalini – Psychosis or Transcendence? Author, 1976, paper.

Schwaller de Lubicz, Isha. Her-Bak, 'Chickpea,' the Living Face of Ancient Egypt. Inner Traditions International, 1978, paper. Her-Bak: Egyptian Initiate. Inner Traditions International, 1978, paper.
The Opening of the Way. Inner Traditions International, 1982, paper.

Schwaller de Lubicz, R. A. The Egyptian Miracle. Inner Traditions International, 1982.
Sacred Science: The King of Pharaonic Theocracy. Inner Traditions International, 1982.
Symbol and Symbolic: Egypt, Science and the Evolution of Consciousness. Autumn Press, 1978, paper.
The Temple in Man: The Secrets of Ancient Egypt. Autumn Press, 1978, paper.

Shearer, Tony. Beneath the Moon and Under the Sun. Sun Books, 1977.
Lord of the Dawn: Quetzalcoatl. Naturegraph, 1971, paper.

Silberer, Herbert. *Hidden Symbolism of Alchemy and the Occult Arts. Dover, 1971, paper. (Also available as Problems of Mysticism and Its Symbolism. Weiser, 1970.)

Three Initiates. *The Kybalion.* DeVorss, 1936.

Toben, Bob. *Space-Time and Beyond.* E. P. Dutton, 1975, paper.

West, John Anthony. *Serpent in the Sky.* Harper & Row, 1979.

White, John, ed. *Kundalini, Evolution and Enlightenment.* Anchor, 1979, paper.

Wilhelm, Richard, and Baynes, Cary F., trans. *The I Ching or Book of Changes.* Princeton University Press, 1967. (Still the best.)

Wilhelm, Richard, trans. *The Secret of the Golden Flower.* Harvest, 1962, paper.

Wolfe, W. Thomas. *And the Sun Is Up: Kundalini Rises in the West.* Academy Hill Press, 1978, paper.

ASTROLOGY

Arroyo, Stephen. *Astrology, Karma & Transformation: The Inner Dimensions of the Birth Chart.* CRCS, 1978, paper.
Astrology, Psychology and the Four Elements. CRCS, 1975, paper.

Bacher, E. *Studies in Astrology,* 9 vols. Rosicrucian Fellowship, 1973, paper.

Bills, Rex. E. *The Rulership Book.* Macoy, 1971.

Carter, Charles E. O. *Astrological Aspects.* Fowler, 1967.
Essays on the Foundations of Astrology. Fowler, 1947.
Principles of Astrology. Theosophical Publishing House, 1969, paper.
Principles of Horoscopic Delineation. Fowler, 1935.

Davison, Ronald C. *Astrology.* Arco, 1963, paper.

Escobar Thyrza. *Essentials of Natal Interpretation.* GSRH, 1973, paper.
The 144 'Doors' of the Zodiac: the Dwad Technique. GSRH, 1974, paper.

Garner, Robert. *What Sign Are You? (Tropical or Sidereal?).* Author, 1971, paper.

Hall, Manly Palmer. *Astrological Keywords.* Littlefield, 1975, paper.

Hand, Robert. *Planets in Transit: Life Cycles for Living.* Para Research, 1976.
Planets in Youth: Patterns of Early Development. Para Research, 1977.

Hickey, Isabel M. *Astrology, A Cosmic Science.* Fellowship House, 1970.

Hickey, Isabel M., and Altieri, Bruce H.
Minerva/Pluto: The Choice is Yours. Altieri Press, 1973, paper.

Holley, Germaine. *Pluto/Neptune: Including Analysis and Inter-pretation of Pisces Duality.* Weiser, 1974, paper.

Jinni and Joanne. *The Digested Astrologer, vol. 1: Signs, Houses, Planets and Aspects.* Authors, 1972, paper.
The Digested Astrologer, vol. 3: The Spiral of Life: Psychological Interpretation. Authors, 1974, paper.

Jones, Marc Edmund. All writings.

Lewi, Grant. *Astrology for the Millions.* Llewellyn, 1969, paper.
Heaven Knows What. Llewellyn, 1976, paper.

Lowell, Laurel. *Pluto.* Llewellyn, 1973, paper.

Mark, Alexandra. *Astrology for the Aquarian Age.* Simon and Schuster, 1970, paper.

Mayo, Jeff. *The Planets and Human Behaviour.* Fowler, 1972.

Meyer, Michael R. *A Handbook for the Humanistic Astrologer.* Anchor, 1974 paper.

Moore, Marcia, and Douglas, Mark. *Astrology, the Divine Science.* Arcane, 1971.

Oken, Alan. *As Above, So Below.* Bantam, 1973, paper.
The Horoscope, the Road and Its Travellers. Bantam, 1974, paper.

Pelletier, Robert. *Planets in Aspect.* Para Research, 1974.

Robertson, Marc. *Time Out of Mind: The Past in Your Astrological Birth Chart and Reincarnation.* Astrology Center of the North-west, 1972, paper.
The Transit of Saturn: Crisis Ages in Adult Life. Astrology Center of the Northwest, 1973, paper.

Rudhyar, Dane. *The Astrological Houses.* Doubleday, 1972, paper.
   An Astrological Mandala. Vintage, 1974, paper.
   Astrological Timing. Harper & Row, 1972, paper.
   The Lunation Cycle. Weiser, 1967, paper.

West, A.W., and Toonder, J.F. *The Case for Astrology.* Penguin, 1970, paper.

Whitman, Edward W. *Aspects and Their Meanings.* Fowler, 1972.
   The Influence of the Houses. Fowler, 1972.
   The Influence of the Planets. Fowler, 1971.

Appendix:
D.O.M.E.
The Inner Guide Meditation Center

We are what we are
and the universe
bursting out of us
contains us too.

From the Neo-Platonists

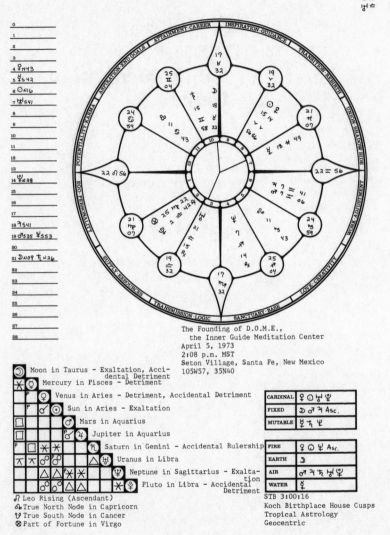

Yod Cross

The Founding of D.O.M.E.,
the Inner Guide Meditation Center
April 5, 1973
2:08 p.m. MST
Seton Village, Santa Fe, New Mexico
105W57, 35N40

Moon in Taurus - Exaltation, Acci-
dental Detriment
Mercury in Pisces - Detriment
Venus in Aries - Detriment, Accidental Detriment
Sun in Aries - Exaltation
Mars in Aquarius
Jupiter in Aquarius
Saturn in Gemini - Accidental Rulership
Uranus in Libra
Neptune in Sagittarius - Exalta-
tion
Pluto in Libra - Accidental
Detriment
Leo Rising (Ascendant)
True North Node in Capricorn
True South Node in Cancer
Part of Fortune in Virgo

CARDINAL	♀ ☉ ♃ ♇
FIXED	☽ ♂ ♄ Asc.
MUTABLE	☿ ♄ ♆

FIRE	♀ ☉ ♆ Asc.
EARTH	☽
AIR	♂ ♃ ♄ ♅ ♇
WATER	☿

STB 3:00:16
Koch Birthplace House Cusps
Tropical Astrology
Geocentric

Natal horoscope of D.O.M.E., The Inner Guide Meditation
Centre.

The Inner Guide Meditation Initiators' Creed of D.O.M.E.

This I know: the flow of universal energies through me and my response to this flow create my personal reality. Bringing myself and these energies into harmony heals my experienced world. The inner worlds generate the outer world, and the source of all is within. The Inner Guides are our teachers and advisors in our personal quest for wholeness and spiritual enlightenment. Work with these inner teachers in the Inner Guide Meditation facilitates achievement of these goals. Each of us carries total responsibility, without blame, for the world that is individually experienced and cannot disclaim responsibility for any portion of it. Work with the Inner Guides can bring this world into a state of harmony and balance. To kill, injure or cause harm, either physical or psychological, to a fellow being injures and causes harm to the individual God-flow. Expansion of individual consciousness expands the consciousness of all beings.

D.O.M.E.
Dei Omnes Munda Edunt

All the Gods
Bring Forth the Worlds/
All the Gods
Eat the Worlds

Excerpts from The Articles of Incorporation and
The Bye-Laws of D.O.M.E.

From the Articles of Incorporation:

1. The name of the corporation is D.O.M.E.

2. The specific and primary purpose of the corporation is to
serve humanity through the foundation and operation of a
centre for the promotion and teaching of the art of living
healthfully, consciously, usefully, spiritually and cooperatively
through the utilization of the Inner Guide Meditation, and in
connection herewith to publish and disseminate literature
concerning these principles and this method of meditation,
and to promote an environment providing the necessary
privacy for spiritual growth where the individual may study
and apply these principles and this method in the context of
the individual's own life and in the context of D.O.M.E. as a
whole.

3. The general purposes of this corporation are exclusively
religious, charitable, scientific, literary and educational within
the meaning of section 501(c)(3) of the Internal Revenue Code
of 1954, and membership shall be open to truthseekers of all

ages, sexes, colours, creeds, races, national origins, sexual preferences, political views and economic states.

9. The duration of the corporation shall be perpetual.

From The By-laws:

Article 1 – Name, Office and Seal
1. Name of the Corporation. The name of the corporation shall be D.O.M.E. The initials 'D.O.M.E.' stand for the Latin phrase *Dei omnes munda edunt.*

Article II – The Purposes and Functions

D.O.M.E., the Inner Guide Meditation Center, is to be an instrument to awaken and increase consciousness, individually and collectively, thereby helping its members and all other beings to achieve a more complete awareness of their position in the structure of the universe through the integration of the individual's manifold nature into one harmonious whole operating at the fullest possible potential in all levels of reality. D.O.M.E. through the Inner Guide Meditation provides a method by which the individual may realize a more creative and harmonious life for himself and his fellow beings. The foundation shall encourage, through the centre founded and operated towards these ends, the pursuit of studies and disciplines leading to the fulfullment of these purposes and shall make known by various and diverse means to interested groups and individuals, ways leading to this fulfillment. In furtherance of such purposes, it shall have the additional purposes and powers to receive and administer funds for religious, scientific, literary, educational and charitable purposes, and for no other purposes, and, to that end, as limited by the following:

1. To establish teaching centres, especially for instruction in the Inner Guide Meditation, philosophy, psychology, comparative religion, the sacred arts, natural laws, metaphysics and the arts and sciences relating to these, of a non-sectarian, non-dogmatic nature, which shall be open to all;

2. To establish and carry on lectures, workshops, classes and seminars of instruction (for both the general public and for students working toward certificates of accomplishment)

where persons may obtain experience and sound instruction relating to physical, mental, emotional and spiritual development and general education of the highest standards, and to manifest, sponsor and promote those activities, including music, art, travel, film, theatre, television, health, energy and agriculture, which are in accordance and consistant with the goals and purposes of D.O.M.E.;

4. To establish and to carry on the services and functions of a meditation, teaching and spiritual centre . . . in any . . . city, county or township of the United States of America, or in any foreign country or countries;

5. To prepare students for ordination as Initiators of the Inner Guide Meditation, *Initiators* having the rights and privileges of a priest, priestess, minister, rabbi, pastor or shaman of any other religious order, and to award the proper certificates or diplomas, on either an honorary or earned basis, evidencing this accomplishment;

7. To collect, preserve and own books, manuscripts, charts, maps, recordings, art and other materials which may be deemed worthy of a place in its archives or museum, and particularly those relating to physical, mental, emotional and spiritual development;

8. To establish a research library and other research facilities relating to physical, mental, emotional and spiritual development consistent with the goals and purposes of D.O.M.E. and to make the results of all published research available to the public at large;

9. To establish a research foundation making the accumulated wisdom of all ages, past, present or future, available to those desiring to partake thereof;

11. To empower *Initiators* and other qualified D.O.M.E. members (as determined by the Board of Trustees) to perform marriage, funeral, dedication and other religious services.

D.O.M.E. Requirements for an Inner Guide Meditation Initiation

Data Required

Date, place and exact *time* of birth. As the horoscope changes basically *every four minutes*, the reading can only be as accurate as the time given. Please try to obtain the time from the *hospital* or from State, County or City *birth records* (not *certificates*). Request a *Full Copy* if sending off to the State for your birth record, and note whether the recorded time is Daylight or Standard Time (especially for births in Illinois, Indiana, Iowa, Michigan and Pennsylvania). Try not to rely on parents' memories, unless the birth time was recorded in a diary or family bible at the time of the birth. Newspaper announcements at the time of birth often include the birthtime. If you cannot obtain your birthtime, a general horoscope for the day can be done and the Inner Guide Meditation initiated, but specific life details will not be available. (An additional charge of $20 is requested for unknown birthtime charts or for changes made in the birth data after the chart has been calculated because of the extra work.)

The First Session

During the initial session, half of the ninety minutes is allotted to an explanation of the horoscope as a map of the inner and outer world experiences. Relatives are 'plugged in' to specific areas of the pattern, and their functions as 'barometers' of those areas is explained. It is useful to have the correct pregnancy or fathering order of your relatives' (mother's, father's, grandparents', brothers', aunts' in-laws', etc.) pregnancies and children fathered for this if it is possible to obtain this information accurately. Miscarriages and abortions

count as a pregnancy, and *where* they occurred in the sequence
is needed. (Birth dates are unnecessary.) Twins count as two
pregnancies, and which twin was first-born is needed. By
'barometers' is meant that the indicated relatives *as their ego
personalities are perceived by you* (how they react to and deal with
the events in their lives in your judgement) will function to show
you how you are dealing with that area of your own life for
which they act as a symbol. To be a barometer has only to do
with how *you* judge them to be dealing with events and
problems.

We will also deal with problem centres in the natal pattern
and those elements which act as causative agents for them.
Coming cycles are discussed, and current problem structures
are pointed out with solutions being suggested. Talents and
capabilities are mentioned and questions are answered. (Make
a list of your questions prior to the session and bring it with
you to insure that none are missed.)

During the second half of the session, the Inner Guide
Meditation is initiated. It is recommended that no drugs
(especially marijuana) be taken eight days prior to this
initiation and that alcohol not be used on the day of the session
itself, as they interfere with the concentration and may prevent
the Guide contact. The first Inner Guide is contacted and
several of the archetypal energy forms are worked with, as is
the Shadow figure. Questions about the Inner Guides and the
meditation are answered and the Worksheet is explained. (It is
useful to have read the book, *The Inner Guide Meditation*, prior to
the initial session.)

Further Sessions

It is generally useful to have daily or weekly sessions until you
feel that the contact with your Inner Guide is well enough
established to continue the inner work on your own. It varies
with the individual as to the number of further sessions
required, three being the average. Many people choose to
have another session or a series of sessions to get back into
working with their Guides if a period of time with no inner
work as such has elapsed or if contact with the Inner Guide has
become tenuous. A series of meditation sessions is sometimes
desirable to accelerate the life change process, to overcome
resistance patterns or to work on the development of some

specific talent or ability. (Bring two 60-minute cassette tapes to each session to record it.)

D.O.M.E. Services

Calculated Horoscopes (using the Koch Birthplace House Cusp System and Tropical, Geocentric Astrology) with **Astrology-Tarot Equivalent Worksheets** and a **Personal Transit Sheets** may be ordered from D.O.M.E. Services, P.O. Box 25358, Colorado Springs, Colorado 80936, U.S.A. The cost is $20 (U.S. dollars). (This includes no interpretation of the horoscope.) See 'Requirements for the Inner Guide Meditation Initiation'.

The Director and Staff of D.O.M.E., the Inner Guide Meditation Center, are available to travel to your area for lectures, seminars, classes, workshops and private Inner Guide Initiation sessions. Inquiries should be made to The Secretary, D.O.M.E., P.O. Box 25358, Colorado Springs, Colorado 80936, U.S.A.

About the Author

Edwin Charles Steinbrecher, originator and developer of the Inner Guide Meditation and founder and director of D.O.M.E. Center, is a second generation astrologer-metaphysician. He is editor of *Aquarian Changes,* D.O.M.E.'s quarterly journal, and a frequent travelling lecturer on the Inner Guide Meditation. He lives and works at D.O.M.E. Center in Colorado Springs, Colorado, where he and his colleagues endeavour to refine and perfect the meditation and to train initiators. His other interests are art, music, film and collage.

Photograph of the author by David Philip Benge.

INDEX